On IMPOSTURE

ON IMPOSTURE

Jean-Jacques Rousseau,
Literary Lies, and Political Fiction

Serge Margel
Translated by Eva Yampolsky

INDIANA UNIVERSITY PRESS

This book is a publication of

Indiana University Press
Office of Scholarly Publishing
Herman B Wells Library 350
1320 East 10th Street
Bloomington, Indiana 47405 USA

iupress.org

Originally published as
De l'imposture: Jean-Jacques Rousseau. Mensonge littéraire et fiction politique
By Serge Margel
Copyright Éditions Galilée, 2007

Manufactured in the United States of America

First printing 2023

Cataloging information is available from the Library of Congress.

ISBN 978-0-253-06529-2 (hardback)
ISBN 978-0-253-06530-8 (ebook)

CONTENTS

FOREWORD

JEAN-JACQUES ROUSSEAU FAMOUSLY CLAIMED TO BELIEVE IN A worldwide plot that aimed to discredit him by besmirching his reputation, accusing him of all manner of crimes—in short, persecuting him. He made such claims nowhere more obsessively than in an odd text written toward the end of his life and published posthumously: *Rousseau, Judge of Jean-Jacques*, known more often as the *Dialogues*. These dialogues are staged between a nameless, featureless Frenchman and someone called "Rousseau," while their only subject of discussion is a third party, "Jean-Jacques," who never speaks directly and never becomes present to the interlocutors. At no point are these two parts of the proper name reconnected to form the same name for a same individual, Jean-Jacques Rousseau, which is nevertheless the name of the one who *presumably* signs the work for all three of the characters. I say "presumably" because, as readers, we can only presume as to the authenticity, veracity, and thus authority of an author's signature. It is this condition of presumptive belief in authority that, according to Serge Margel, Rousseau would have understood and denounced as an imposture, not only in this late text but across his life's work.

Rousseau scholars often minimize reference to the *Dialogues*, which can indeed read like a maddening exercise in paranoid schizophrenia. Not surprisingly, this work has rarely been reedited over the past 250 years, and then usually only in editions of Rousseau's complete works rather than as a free-standing text, unlike the *Confessions* or the *Social Contract*, to name just two endurably popular works by Rousseau. But then in 1962, Michel Foucault, at the time known above all as the author of the massive *History of Madness* that had been published a year earlier, was asked to write a preface for an edition of the *Dialogues*, perhaps on the expectation that he would diagnose its author's delusion or at least situate it in the history of madness that interested him. If so, Foucault disappointed with a brilliant essay that mined many new insights and concluded with a brief dialogue of its own, kicked off by an interlocutor who asks rather skeptically: "So the *Dialogues* are not the work of a madman?" To which comes a cryptic reply from, let us presume, the author of the essay just concluded: "This question would matter if it made any sense. The work, by definition, is non-madness." But the skeptic persists: "The structure of a work can allow the pattern of madness to appear," which is met by a no less cryptic response: "What is decisive is that the reciprocal assertion is not true."[1] In other words, it is not true that a pattern of madness can allow the structure of a work to appear. Ipso facto and by definition, the work is non-madness.

It seems to me that Margel would not disagree with that assertion. And not only because he quotes here several times from the *Dialogues* and always to bring home a point about the lucidity of "Rousseau," the lucidity not of a man but of a signed work. How, you ask, can a work be lucid? In the sense, perhaps, that it illuminates or illustrates itself as disembodied thought, as proper name split off from the finite, mortal, individual body that bore the name and that is then what Margel calls *désœuvré*, unworked. According to Margel, Rousseau's work is lucid about this condition of the proper name that survives the bearer, that lives on as a site for the projections of readers who thereby *impose* themselves as, in effect, authors of what they read. A reader's imposture, then, is no less insidious than an author's.

By his own confession, Rousseau was an inveterate impostor, in the most common sense of the word. He recounts in the *Confessions* several episodes where he assumed a false identity, claimed another's experience, or used an alias.[2] These episodes are sometimes told with a sense of their folly, and rarely are they occasions to express any regret for the deception perpetrated. Although Margel does not bring this confessed experience of an impostor anywhere into the foreground of his reading, it manages to signal from the wings of his analysis, like a tacit symptom taking direction of the cure, as Jacques Lacan would say.[3] I venture this analogy between Margel's practice here with Rousseau's text and the scene of the "talking cure" to give some account of a striking quality of *Of Imposture*: its attention to what suffers and writes from out of that suffering. It is, to be sure, not manifestly the quality of some pathos or sympathy, but rather a capacity to let the text proclaim its innocence and let it be believed. This quality is perhaps nowhere more in evidence than in the meticulous unpacking of Rousseau's famous lie of the stolen ribbon, recounted first in the *Confessions* and reexamined a few years later in his *Reveries of the Solitary Walker*. With his analysis, Margel is able to clear a ground here for the possibility of the "kind of lie [that] is purely innocent."[4]

Although Rousseau may have inaugurated a tradition of modern autobiography, especially with his *Confessions*, it was his political treatises that registered the greatest impact on his own age, as well as a devastating effect on their author's life when both the *Social Contract* and *Emile, or On Education*, were publicly burned and Rousseau was forced to flee under an arrest warrant. Catholic authorities in Paris and Protestant ones in Rousseau's birthplace, Geneva, were the forces behind this suppression of what they recognized as dangerous to their exclusive say over religious belief and, beyond that and more important, their hold over temporal power. As regards the *Social Contract*, it was the penultimate chapter, "Civil Religion," that had especially to be banned and burned, for, among other affronts, asserting that Christianity "is more harmful than useful to the strong constitution of the state."[5] It is most harmful wherever it forms a body that can rule not just alongside but with power over the body of civil society and its government. The temporal power of those who profess to concern themselves only with the salvation of souls for the extratemporal world is, once again, the sort of *imposture* that Rousseau continued to expose, as Margel shows, ever since his early writing on the origin of inequality.

It should be said that this word "imposture" has a somewhat different extension in English than in French, where it is more clearly related to a verb, *imposer*, which itself has many common senses and uses. But the most pertinent here is an idiomatic use, *en imposer (à quelqu'un)*, for which the best English translation is "to impress (someone)." An impostor impresses, imposes on the credulous, which makes imposture the primary tool not just of the priest but of the legislator. Christians, this chapter of the *Social Contract* argues, are especially vulnerable to such imposition not necessarily because they are more credulous but rather—at least if they are good Christians and not something akin to impostors—because, as Rousseau has it, "Christian charity does not easily allow one readily to think ill of one's neighbor." This charity is fertile ground, then, for an impresser, imposer, or impostor who, like Catiline or Cromwell, "As soon as he has found, through some ruse, the art of impressing them [*de leur en imposer*] and of seizing a share of public authority, there he is, behold, a man given honors whom God wills you to respect."[6] This is a replay of what Margel calls, in the book's opening pages, the "archaic scene," which Rousseau had first reconstructed in his *Discourse on the Origin and Foundations of Inequality*, and which continues to be repeated and restaged, with different actors, across all the ages of human society. Like some Catiline or Cromwell (but the list is long and examples are never lacking), that man who "having fenced off a plot of ground, took it into his head to say *this is mine* and found people simple enough to believe him, was the true founder of civil society."[7] For Margel every word counts in these renowned lines, and he doesn't overlook any of their implications (or impositions), in particular, the feature of a performative speech act masked as a constative assertion that merely states or deictically points to what *is* the case: "*this is mine.*" Such would have been the archaic scene of imposing, impressing, or impostoring, to supply a verb that English lacks. Rousseau goes on to say that such an event could have taken place only after many earlier ideas had been acquired, and there had been much progress before arriving at this point he designates as the origin of civil society and therefore as the end of the state of nature. Of these developments, the most significant—in both senses of the word—was the invention of language. For, as Margel acutely observes, "without being *linked* to a discourse that imposes their veracity, these borders [on a plot of ground] in themselves have no meaning, no effect, nor reality."[8] Veracity is an attribute not of things but of language, and here it is plainly the effect of a performative imposition or imposture.

Language: Ay, there's the rub, the archi-impostor.

I mentioned that Rousseau frequently played the impostor throughout his life. But he also suffered, he claimed, from an inability to impose himself and impress others with witty conversation in society, especially in the society of women. He thus learned to prefer to be alone and to write, where words seemed to come easily and to flow into memorable rhetorical rhythms. It is as if Rousseau the writer could throw off all imposture, at last.

Peggy Kamuf
Los Angeles, June 2021

Notes

1. Michel Foucault, introduction to *Rousseau juge de Jean-Jacques: Dialogues*, by Jean-Jacques Rousseau (Paris: Armand Colin, 1962), xxiv, my translation, http://1libertaire.free.fr/MFoucault247.html.

2. On these impostures, see Geoffrey Bennington, *Dudding: Des noms de Rousseau* (Paris: Galilée, 1991).

3. See Jacques Lacan, "The Direction of the Treatment and the Principles of Its Power," in *Écrits*, trans. Bruce Fink (New York: Norton, 2007), 489–542.

4. See "*Mendacium est fabula*, or The Right to Lie by Admission of Innocence," 9.

5. Jean-Jacques Rousseau, *Du contrat social*, vol. 3 of *Œuvres complètes*, ed. Bernard Gagnebin and Marcel Raymond, Bibliothèque de la Pléiade (Paris: Gallimard, 1964), 464, my translation.

6. Ibid., 466.

7. Jean-Jacques Rousseau, *Discourse on the Origin and Foundations of Inequality among Men*, in *The First and Second Discourses*, ed. Roger D. Masters, trans. Roger D. Masters and Judith R. Masters (Boston: Bedford/St. Martin's, 1964), 141.

8. See "Introduction: The Staging of an Imposture," 3.

ON IMPOSTURE

INTRODUCTION:
THE STAGING OF AN IMPOSTURE

For the present I should like merely to understand how it happens that so many men, so many villages, so many cities, so many nations, sometimes suffer under a single tyrant who has no other power than the power they give me.

Étienne de La Boétie, *The Discourse on Voluntary Servitude*

§ 1 "WHAT IS LITERATURE?" "WHAT IS POLITICS?" In Rousseau's works the literary and the political are inseparable to the point of confusion. These two questions cannot be raised separately; however, we can analyze, situate, and reconstruct the place where these two questions appear and intersect. In this text I will try to define this place as the archaic scene of an imposture. This scene leads to the problems of lying, trickery, and betrayal, which threaten not only literal or textual meaning but also power, law, and authority. As in theater, a liar is an actor, sometimes as a *reader* who deciphers and interprets the meaning of a text and the meaning of the world and sometimes as a *legislator* who defines the rules of the game and justifies the reasons for the scene. However, this archaic scene is not an original or primal one, inscribed in the "nature" of humans and society. In reality, it is at once archaic and constructed. It is archaic in the sense that it concerns the *archè*, the principle or the source, but which has no specified origin or assigned place. This scene cannot be situated, nor even dated and inscribed in a particular period in history. It is constructed in the sense that it is produced and conceived of according to specific rules. On the one hand, it is constructed or made up, as one would make up a story, and on the other hand, it is staged, in the sense of staging a play. In a way it is thus the place of a paradox or, more specifically, the paradoxical place where the questions of the literary and the political play out and interconnect.

Therefore, this archaic scene of imposture has never existed; it has never been played out, represented, named, or signed. In a certain sense, this scene does not exist, but it can nonetheless be reconstructed. This is precisely what this essay will attempt to do, in and with Rousseau's texts. Not only does imposture, as a term or at least as a notion, appear throughout his works, from the first *Discourse* to the *Social Contract*, from the *Confessions* to *Emile*, up to the *Reveries*, but more importantly it is precisely this term that allows Rousseau to address, define, and critique the great questions of the literary and the political. However, for Rousseau, the question of the literary is founded on the figure of the reader, in the same way that the political is founded on the figure of the legislator. We could go so far as to claim that literature itself is a question or the problem of the reader. It is the reader who determines the meaning, who chooses, judges and drives the text, to the point of inventing the ambivalent figure of the author. Literature is a form of reading, or a certain type of discourse that, in Rousseau's terms, is always "interested" and that determines the conditions of the legibility of a text. It is thus a normative and dominant discourse that alone constitutes and imposes the categories of the literary field, its various genres, the opposition between reality and fiction, and especially the internal division of the author between an individual body and a proper name. In this sense, it is the reader who establishes the literary space by dividing the individual from within, in order to appropriate the identity behind the name and to create the institution of authorship. According to Rousseau, it is the same case with the legislator, who alone represents and embodies the question of the political. It is the legislator who establishes the common laws of society and, more importantly, compels the subject, from within, to follow these laws. It is also the legislator who, all at once, divides the subject into a private being and a public entity, an individual body and a collective body, forcing adherence to a right to inequality and thus submission to the most powerful, or to the authority of a dominant discourse.

The reader and the legislator thus represent the two major figures of the impostor, whom Rousseau situates at the origin of every society and attempts to attribute to what he calls the transition from nature to culture, or to society. In other words, for Rousseau, the principle of every society is founded on imposture, or on a specific imposture, which allows humanity to radically differentiate or distinguish itself from animality. In any case, this is where the archaic scene is conceived and constructed, which establishes a new order of reality—society, culture, and history—and creates the framework for perpetual war: the right to inequality, to destitution and murder, but also to deceit and lying.

> The first person who, having fenced off a plot of ground, took it into his head to say *this is mine* and found people simple enough to believe him, was the true founder of civil society. What crimes, wars, murders, what miseries and horrors would the human race have been spared by someone who, uprooting the stakes or filling in the ditch, had shouted to his fellows: Beware of listening to this impostor; you are lost if you forget that the fruits belong to all and the Earth to no one! But it is very likely that by then things had already come to the point where they could no longer remain as they were. For this idea of

property, depending on many prior ideas which could only have arisen successively, was not conceived all at once in the human mind. It was necessary to make much progress, to acquire much industry and enlightenment, and to transmit and augment them from age to age, before arriving at this last stage of the state of Nature.[1]

Once again, if this founding scene is not rooted in history in the strict sense, it is nonetheless in the consequent course of progress, in the elaboration of a trajectory, in the construction of a form that appears, one day, in the performative speech of a man who "took it into his head to say *this is mine.*" This "idea of property," with its right and legitimacy, is not founded on the enclosure he creates or on the ditch he digs, nor on the establishment or institution of delimitations, barriers, or borders. Without being *linked* to a discourse that imposes their veracity, these borders in themselves have no meaning, no effect, no reality. They do not delimit anything without a discourse that declares: "this is mine." However, we must be wary of falling, once again, into the trap of discourse. For if there are no borders without a discourse or property without performative speech to express it, there will also be no discourse to declare itself and to begin the performance of the first scene without those to whom this discourse is addressed. According to Rousseau, there is no discourse without there being someone to listen to it, to adhere or to submit to it, and to believe it. Saying "this is mine" means nothing, at least *not yet*, if it is not believed by those who hear it.

In other words, for a society to be established and for the social principle to be founded, it does not suffice to simply enclose a site, to put up barriers, or even to assert or defend a right to property. First and foremost, one must find "people simple enough" to believe in it. In other words, it is those who are simple, naive, or imbeciles who give legitimacy to the discourse of borders and thus the validity of the notion of property. For it is this figure of listening, of address, and of belief that is essential to the archaic creation of the imposture and the *foundation* of its scene. The reality of borders is created or established by those who believe in the discourse of borders. In this sense, these are ultimately the true founders of civil society. The belief of "simple individuals" does not bear on the declaration of an imposture, for it does not recognize its already established reality; rather, it is their belief itself that establishes its reality. This belief makes the first human who imposes borders a true impostor. It is precisely and only this belief that sets the stage for the first and immortal imposture. Yet what does this notion of "belief" mean here, and how are we to define its status, function, and role in the archaic construction of its own scene?

§ 2 The scene of the first imposture is thus not founded on borders, nor even on its discourse, but rather on a certain belief that *links* this discourse to the borders, as one can link knowledge to power, in order to establish the authority of a dominant discourse. In this sense, "[finding] people simple enough to believe him" implies finding *accomplices* to establish power or to form an association of impostors. Without the elaboration of a *plot*, there could be no imposture, no power or dominant discourse, no established and instituted political body. It is not a question of a gathering of militant accomplices or a mob of partisans committed to the same cause, but rather that of a plot by simpleminded individuals who are not aware of the impostor's position. They did not realize that the impostor's strategy—and thus his imposture—consists in the *fabrication of the accomplice*. This fabrication, like a factory or a machine, only seeks to produce a diversion from the imposture. Its goal is not only to dissimulate places, dates, and identities and to erase the signs and various traces of the event but, more importantly, to divert attention from and render invisible, unintelligible, or simply inaccessible the institutional reconstruction of an imposture. Rousseau describes this in terms of a transition from the initial and archaic imposture to the instituted power of a valid, legal, and legitimate appropriation.

The figure of the accomplice, without which this transition would be inconceivable, unrealizable, impossible, is nonetheless a tragic one, which only exists and whose sole reason to exist is to be the product of an imposture and *at the same time* to produce an imposture. Considering this, the figure of the accomplice itself represents the strategic stance taken by the impostor in order to dissimulate the imposture, to divert or to establish it as a right to property. This is the stance that the first creator of borders must have adopted to transform this imposture into a "right to inequality." This strategic stance of complicity, clandestine and silent, dubious and secret, but also tragic, is adopted by those without whom none of the experienced ordeals, suffering, and misery would have become a necessary part of humanity. In other words, the figure of the accomplice represents a barrier, an obstacle, perhaps even a mirage, but a necessary and defining one. This figure exists not only to establish civil society, along with its institutions of inequality, from the family to the school, from the prison to the hospital, but also and more importantly to veil, to conceal, to render inaccessible or even unrepresentable the entire fraudulent strategy on which societies are founded.

For Rousseau, however, this figure of the accomplice has two exemplary faces, or two dominant sides. The *legislator*, on the one hand, validates authority, justifies power, and legitimizes the right to inequality among people by distinguishing the individual body from the collective one. The *reader*, on the other hand, imposes the norms of meaning, the criteria of interpretation, and the conditions of legibility by dividing the human from within into an individual body and a proper name. Here, these two faces of complicity, these two imposturous plots thus create the space for an infinite scope of the political and the literary. Yet the reason for this tragic notion of culture, society, and history lies not only in having inscribed the political and the literary within the space from which the first imposture emerged, but also in inextricably linking them, for the return of an immutable imposture. If politics does not exist, has never existed, and will never exist without literature, nor does literature exist without politics, then it is directly and entirely because of this exchange, this economy that shares an imposture. In other words, there can be no politics or literature without an imposture that defines them from the inside and establishes their meaning. At the same time, however, an imposture cannot be instituted without politics and literature, which establish an order of legitimization and fiction, or a legitimizing fiction whose objective is the indefinite, invisible, and silent reproduction or the *return* of the initial and immortal imposture. Once again, this archaic scene of imposture does not exist as such, but only in its indefinite ability to come back to restructure the field of discourse. Yet this return is indiscernible, masked, encrypted, encoded, for it never appears in its true form and never utters its own name. This return makes it seem as if that which returns had always already been there. For Rousseau, however, this is a meticulously planned trap, set up by a systematic reconstruction of the impostors' eternal plot. This collective fraud, which has become secular, thwarts all future, all memory, and all testimonial hope for a future. Any form of address, even a future and ideal one; any word, sentence, or text, even if it is addressed to a "disinterested," ideal or future reader, would already be contaminated, corrupted, or simply invested in by the murderous necessity to recreate the scene of this first imposture, which is at the foundation of society, culture, and history.

Yet this new literary space of "unworking" evoked by Rousseau emerges precisely from this situation, this inescapable state.[2] Indeed, the return to this ultimate point of the imposture is not only a question of examining and critiquing the political conditions that make a text, or the text, legible, but it is also and especially a question of transforming this critique or crisis into the possibility of relating literature to unworking or, more specifically, of drawing the literary out of the unworking. In short, the denunciation of this crisis is no longer a question of reducing the literary to the sole figure of the reader, to his or her authority and identity, in the objective of creating meaning and understanding. Rather, it is the ability to make this crisis emerge directly from the expropriation of the name, from the dispossession of the body and the overthrow of figures of authority. It is thus a question of reducing all forms of legibility, meaning, and interpretation to the *loss* of identity, authority, and specificity, ultimately in order to be able to reduce the legible to the illegible foundation that shapes it from within. In this sense, it is the beginning of another scene, whose objective is to create an anonymous body, one that is unworked, dispossessed, deprived not only of its body parts and movements, of its possessions and virtues, but also and more importantly of everything that defines it as an individual body, its name, its honor, and its life. This is the possibility of a new framework of a political inscription of a *body without a name*, without memory or future, from which a new literary dimension of reading and writing can emerge.

Notes

1. Jean-Jacques Rousseau, *Discourse on the Origin and Foundations of Inequality among Men (Second Discourse)*, vol. 3 of *The Collected Writings of Rousseau*, ed. Roger D. Masters and Christopher Kelly, trans. Judith R. Bush, Roger D. Masters, Christopher Kelly, and Terrence Marshall (Hanover, NH: University Press of New England, 1992), 43.

2. [I have translated the terms *désœuvrement* and *désœuvré* as "unworking" and "unworked" throughout.—Trans.]

MENDACIUM EST FABULA, OR THE RIGHT TO LIE BY ADMISSION OF INNOCENCE

Jean-Jacques Rousseau: From the Fourth Walk to the Epigraph of the Confessions

Just as we have investigated what mouth is referred to in the quotation:
"The mouth that belieth, killeth the soul,"
so we may ask what type of lie is indicated.

Augustine, *Lying*, 33

Introduction

When I confess something to someone or to God, what kind of speech act am I making? What is the nature of this act, and how can the event that this act involves, engages, or promises be described? I would like to show that in Rousseau's texts, according to one hypothesis, the act of confessing constitutes the paradigm of all speech acts, a dynamic form that both establishes and problematizes a double discursive structure. This traditional double opposition consists of *truth and lies* on the one hand and *the author and the reader* on the other. The first opposition concerns the notion of *reference*: what does a confession say? Does it consist of information, judgment, or knowledge, and, in this last case, what kind of knowledge are we confronted with? Can it be verified, proven, confirmed, and objectively identified, enough to persuade that the confessed discourse is not simply the utterance of a lie, just as one might with a purely informative or semiotic speech act? Certainly not, for its value of truth is a "total truth," one that cannot be reduced to the level of a directly identifiable, manifest, or explicit reference (as it could be done with a fact or even an expressed feeling). The function of a lie in the act of confessing, a question that will be examined here, would no longer be defined simply as the opposite of truth, but rather as its indiscernible double, its indelible shadow. The second couple—the author and the reader—deals with the figure of the *addressee*: who is speaking in a confession and whom does this discourse address? For Rousseau, every intended or designated reader, every interpreter, every creator of a body of work necessarily accomplishes a reading that is partial and unfaithful but also biased, tendentious, and interested. A reader is thus defined as a kind of anonymous, masked avenger, a spy whose critical, hermeneutic discourse will raise the suspicion of being an imposture and whose very own subjective neutrality and strictest objectivity are threatened. Nonetheless, one needs to address the reader, and thus to presume his or her existence, while at the same time inventing, formulating, positioning the reader as an author and a creator of his or her reading.[1] Yet this postulate is not that of a defined and stable identity, but rather a position of conflict between the author's presumed identity and his or her authority as an imposture.[2]

According to Rousseau, the act of confessing takes place within the traditional opposition of lies and truth. It is not a question of *telling* the truth, and thus of running the unavoidable risk of lying, but of telling the *whole* truth—of sacrificing oneself *for* the truth to the limits of innocence. One might think that this powerful desire to "say everything" consists in rectifying the judgment of the other, in convincing or persuading them, in seeking their approval or in asking for their forgiveness.[3] Yet this question is much more radical. It does not suffice to explain to the reader one's most minute actions with the sole purpose of self-justification. Rather, it is a question of interrupting the reading or interpretation, of rendering it impossible by transforming the confessed narrative into an *illegible* discourse. There would thus be nothing left to read or to say. Everything would become illegible, not in the sense of being dissimulated, encrypted, encoded, but because this "everything" that is confessed will have always already been exhausted, interpreted, read, narrated, and *sovereignly* judged. Everything will have been confessed not before God but under God's scrutiny. And given the fact that everything will be said in accordance with the verdict of the Last Judgment, the reader, deprived [*désœuvré*] of their own reading, would only be able to admit their innocence. This type of confession would be neither juridical (the declaration of one's innocence) nor psychological (the recognition of innocence) but rather an admission that we could qualify as being hermeneutic. At the same time, this confession is an admission *of* the reader's own unworking and the admission *as* a form of unworking—a destiny that is "proper" to the reader. Rousseau repeats it time and again: one must either admit or deceive, mask, disfigure, and slander. However, necessary as it may be, this confession is nonetheless impossible. It is necessary in order to avoid discrediting God's judgment but also impossible because this imposture is the condition for the existence of the critical identity and authority of the reader. For the reader, who is now unworked, *reading* is no longer a question of *interpreting* or *composing* a literary work but merely that of *bearing witness to* his or her own unworking by making an admission of innocence.

In order to show how this confession of innocence, that of a confessed discourse, relates to the testimony of silence, that of God before the text of the *Confessions*, I will first analyze the structure of a lie inherent to all enunciations. I will then explain how this structure needed to be effaced literally as pure fiction in the act of confessing. For this reason, it will be necessary to relate the well-known lie in the scene of the stolen ribbon in book 2 of the *Confessions* to the Fourth Walk of the *Reveries of the Solitary Walker*, a kind of confession of the *Confessions*, as Paul de Man put it, a veritable justification by which the causes and the effects of the lie had to be described, and by which at the same time a lie existing within all discourse and beyond all judgment had to be confirmed.[4] This kind of lie is purely innocent.

I. Lying in the *Confessions*: Between Innocence and Injustice

Testimony, Lies, and Truth

§ 1 The objective of Rousseau's *Confessions* is to tell *all* the truth. But what kind of truth? Is there a single person who can measure the confessed truth in its entirety? If so, that person would be neither judge nor advocate, neither accuser nor confessor, but simply a *witness*. According to the epigraph of the *Confessions*, it is the reader who must first and foremost bear witness. One might then ask why this is and thus question the pertinence of and the reason for placing the reader in the position of a witness by the one who confesses. In this case the value of the truth of a confession depends directly on the recognition of the witness. The one who confesses would then play the role of the accused, while the witness would have the power to judge. In this case, however, the utterance of confessions would be entirely submitted to the juridical order. Yet Rousseau does not neglect to state that "being just is not enough to be innocent." But how does one judge this innocence? How can one legitimize a confessed discourse that no longer consists in nor is reduced to telling the truth, and thus to being just, which instead commits to telling *all* the truth and, as we will see, to presenting its innocence? In reality, no such justice exists that can evaluate or assess innocence. There would be neither accusation nor defense nor denegation nor recognition, but simply an *admission*—an admission of innocence made by the presumed author of the *Confessions* that the reader bears witness to, the epigraph of which I will now quote in its entirety:

This the only portrait of a man, painted exactly according to nature and in all its truth, that exists and will probably ever exist. Whoever you may be, whom destiny or my trust has made the arbiter of the fate of these notebooks, I entreat you, in the name of my misfortunes, of your compassion, and of all human kind, not to destroy a unique and useful work, which may serve as a first point of comparison in the study of man that certainly is yet to be begun, and not to take away from the honour of my memory the only sure monument to my character that has not been disfigured by my enemies. Finally, were you yourself to be one of those implacable enemies, cease to be so towards my ashes, and do not pursue your cruel injustice beyond the term both of my life and yours; so that *you might for once present the noble evidence* of having been generous and good, when you might have been wicked and vindictive; if, that is, the evil directed at a man who has never himself done nor wanted to do any could properly bear the name of vengeance.[5]

This epigraph merits in-depth study, but I will content myself with noting that the "noble evidence" [*témoignage*] in question here concerns not the "author" of the *Confessions* but the reader. Furthermore, it is not a question of giving a witness account of something *to* someone, nor even of admitting something *about* someone. Instead, it is a question of testifying *to oneself*—a testimony of goodness, generosity, and grace. But what does it mean to be the witness of one's own grace, like a sublime witness?[6] If Rousseau had wanted to use this epigraph simply to take the reader as a witness, this testimony would have been nothing more than a confessional call for forgiveness. However, we are not taking the reader as a witness nor asking for his or her forgiveness; rather, we are asking the reader to bear witness to his or her own grace. This is precisely what I would call an admission of innocence, to which I will return more in depth. The challenge of this admission lies in confusing, through a subtle but highly violent tour de force, the *testimony of grace* and the *purity of innocence*. The reader would need to be disconcerted, confused, even accused of false testimony, to the point that the generosity of his or her heart transforms into self-testimony; to the point that the reader admits that every reference to an unjust act could only have derived from his or her own desire for an imposture. More specifically, the form that this testimony had to take *clears* the author's juridical responsibility of any moral crime. It converts the committed injustice into an *error* of justice, of reading or interpretation, and creates at the heart of all condemnations the testimonial structure of an admission. The reader's role will thus not be to *judge* the author, or to recognize the author's identity within his or her guilt, but rather to admit to a desire for imposture by bearing witness to innocence.

This strange economy of testimony will allow me to distinguish between the *just* and the *innocent* or, more precisely, between two concepts of innocence, and thus two types of injustice. One would be strictly juridical, by which the summoning of witnesses would serve to verbally declare the author's guilt or innocence and then to formalize the judgment. The other would not explicitly depend on the juridical order, whereby the call for witnesses would not be possible because there would be no higher authority in place able to hear the position taken by a witness. There will be a witness nonetheless, but a silent one; a witness who says nothing, sees nothing, and hears nothing. This will be a pure witness of grace, blind, deaf, and mute, but most importantly one who is infinitely indebted. This witness will need to admit him or herself that the task at hand is not to make the author innocent, as a witness would in the juridical sense, but rather to establish him or herself as the mournful memory of innocence. This witness would feel guilty for interpreting a work on which God himself would have already brought the judgment of his last gaze. This is what I will later try to define as the false testimony of the reader as witness. For now, however, a question must be asked: how can innocence and injustice as a pair—this primary couple that the *Confessions* constantly underscore—be defined within and beyond judiciary reason?

§ 2 According to Rousseau, there is an act whose innocence and injustice cannot be measured by any form of justice. He describes this act in the *Confessions*, claiming to have committed it himself as an adolescent, when he was Madame Vercellis's lackey in Turin. This act concerns a *lie*, a terrible lie by which he falsely accused "poor Marion," a servant, of stealing "a little ribbon, silver and rose-coloured and already quite old," that he himself took.[7] The narrative of this event, to which I will return later, is of great importance. Throughout his life, this was a source of great pain for Rousseau. He writes: "This burden, then, has lain unalleviated on my conscience until this very day; and I can safely say that the desire to be in some measure relieved of it has greatly contributed to the decision I have taken to write my confessions."[8] This relief must be examined. How did it take place and in what way did the fact of having the reader as witness make the realization of such a deep desire possible?

It is in the Fourth Walk that we can find parts of an answer to this question. Upon reading a treatise by Plutarch (*How to Profit by One's Enemies*) and comparing it to the Abbé Rozier's maxim (*vitam vero impendenti*), Rousseau decides to write a few pages on the question of lying. First, of course, he thought about how he himself lied and accused Marion nearly fifty years earlier. Even though lying is one of the worst acts that Rousseau had committed, this bad act is nonetheless *paradoxical*. His heart was tormented by pain and distress until his death, nonetheless Rousseau states that this act was carried out without "the slightest regret" and without feeling "[any] real remorse."[9] This contradiction is the paradox of lying or, as we will see, the *paradox of an innocent lie*. How can one not regret committing an act that makes one a lifelong victim of endless suffering? More importantly, how does one judge or even confess to this paradox, or to this problem that is among the most difficult to solve in philosophy? "I realized that the accuracy of the judgement that I had to make about myself in this respect depended on the solution to this problem."[10]

On Ethical Value and the Uses of Lying

§ 1 "I remember having read in a work of philosophy that lying is concealing a truth that one must make known."[11] This statement, which brings to mind and perfectly summarizes Plato's, Aristotle's, as well as Saint Augustine's philosophical notions, while also anticipating Kant's severe judgment, involves the three major ethical dimensions of lying: (1) the *epistemic* lie—lying is possible only by the one who *knows* the truth; (2) the *strategic* lie—a liar is someone who uses the lie as a means to *deceive* another person, either to *cause harm* or to *protect* the other's soul or body from some misfortune; (3) the *transcendental* lie—a liar is a person who does not spontaneously obey the imperative by which everyone has the *duty* to tell the truth.[12]

In a philosophical discourse, lying is therefore the act of "*concealing* a *truth* that one *must* make known." First, Rousseau turns his attention to the notion of duty. For instance, if I give counterfeit money to someone to whom I do not owe anything, I am doubtlessly deceiving them, but I am not stealing from them. At first glance, if nothing forces me to tell a truth, or the truth, deception does not constitute a crime. Consequently, concealing the truth would no longer be confused with lying. This leads to two questions. First, under which conditions can one speak of a *truth that is owed*? Second, is the possibility of an *innocent lie* conceivable? Here a strategy is elaborated that does not consist in naively excusing a lie out of kindness but in creating a relation between lying and innocence that no duty to establish the truth and thus no veracity could ever define. This, of course, requires a tour de force. This single problem is formulated in two different ways. It is easy to understand that if truth is not something that is owed, certain lies would be free of injustice. But can we go so far as to call them innocent? Rousseau's intention is not to establish a disgraceful compromise, in the Kantian sense, nor does he wish to allow tolerance for certain deceptive acts out of generosity or humanity. On the contrary, every lie needs to be judged, but judged distinctly. In other words, it would not be a question of reaching a judgment in order to accuse the liar and to condemn him or her for hurting the other or seeing humanity in its essence; rather, it would be a question of arriving at a judgment capable of *effacing* the act of lying itself in the enunciation of the lie. And this, as we will see, is where it becomes necessary for the reader to be called as witness, for an admission of innocence to be possible.

In replying to the first question, Rousseau distinguishes, on the one hand, the general and abstract truth from the particular and individual truth.[13] Here it is not a question of differentiating truth from veracity but theoretical truth from practical truth. On the other hand, Rousseau opposes useful truths—be they theoretical and instructive or practical and effective—to useless truths, ones of no interest or consequence to anyone. From this he infers: "Truth stripped of any kind of usefulness, even possible usefulness, can therefore not be a thing that is owed to anybody, and consequently anyone who conceals or disguises it is not lying."[14] From this conclusion, he then turns immediately to the second question. Even though concealing the truth and saying what is false are two different things, they can produce the same effect, "for this effect is certainly the same whenever it is nil," writes Rousseau.[15] But how is one to understand the term "effect," and even more so the nullity from which this effect *results*? Would we not be defining the degree zero of the effect, a kind of effect without effect, one that has no effect on the other but one that is capable of disturbing the heart to the point where it can no longer differentiate between a silence and a lie? The difficulty would consist in situating and describing, within the heart of the other, this degree zero of a lie. The opposition of two differences would need to be subtly but violently confronted: the distinction between concealing the truth and saying what is false, on the one hand, and the distinction between the act of concealing this truth and keeping silent, on the other. And who would still be able to judge if this indifferent effect is indeed the result of the erasure of difference between two types of silence?

§ 2 When a truth can be considered completely useless, it makes no difference if I affirm or conceal it. But in that case how does one know that in keeping silent one is concealing the truth? In certain extreme situations—in which I could be confronted with the renunciation of my faith or the betrayal of my best friend, for instance—Saint Augustine would advise me to keep silent.[16] But here Rousseau speaks about a different kind of silence. This silence must not be defined as a constraint. It is neither a refusal of speech nor the rejection of an event but rather a simple effect, a state, a disposition of the heart, in which nothing that was supposed to happen will take place. The degree of usefulness of truth will be so nil that any obligation to make it known would already have been discredited. When I no longer owe the truth to anyone, when I am no longer indebted to someone—in other words, following Rousseau's reasoning, when "a person who deceives by telling the opposite of the truth is no more reprehensible than a person who deceives by not telling the truth"—nothing allows me to distinguish between a lie and a silence, and the essence of all the categorical postulates of moral judgment would be *ipso facto* called into question.[17] For if one is not more unjust than the other and if the latter is thus not more just than the first, it is because at this nil level of effect there is no sufficiently authorized justice to accuse the liar of keeping the truth to himself. And this is precisely at this level of insufficiency that Rousseau situates the difference between the just and the innocent.

"If I do no wrong to someone by deceiving them, does it follow that I am doing no wrong to myself, and is it enough never to be unjust in order always to be innocent?"[18] For now, we know nothing about the concept of innocence, or almost nothing, for we already know that the possibility of a degree zero of harm depends on it. However, from this point on, this degree zero can no longer be considered simply in terms of neutrality, as a kind of uncertain origin between the just and the unjust. Instead, it would be a question of a shift between this uncertainty itself and the wrong that I can do to myself. Innocence would thus represent a form of justice or the fairness of judgment toward oneself. But let us be more precise and consider the condition on which the wrong that one might do to oneself can exist beyond one's just conduct toward the other. Even though the effective value of innocence results from this condition, this innocence could no longer be defined as a measure of justice, even of superior justice. Certainly, the wrong that I might do to myself must be judged in terms of innocence rather than with regard to the laws of justice. Nonetheless, innocence will not be a criterion for evaluating such a judgment but rather the state of the sufferer's heart, at once indefinitely deferred and eminently expected. One must find "a reliable rule" to measure the gap, most likely an infinite one, between the just and the innocent.[19]

When I do wrong to no one but myself, what am I doing? Am I lying to myself? Rousseau does not answer this question directly, and while I do not intend to respond for him, we could say nonetheless that only I am capable of measuring the damage caused by this wrong. However, I need a rule, an intimate and personal one; my own rule, unknown to all, yet one that is provided to each and every one of us.[20] Of course at times it can remain silent and let my body fall prey to its passions. Nonetheless, I will never be able to forget it. It will always come to mind like a *memory rule*, for, after all, it is from memory, or from my memory, that I will extract this rule and "the proof of its infallibility."[21] Rousseau writes: "It is then [in my recollections] that I judge myself as severely perhaps as I shall be judged by the supreme judge once this life is over."[22] I find this memory rule, which allows me at any moment to anticipate the Last Judgment, inscribed within me as a "certitude," like the most profound conviction that my heart will have always been right. By judging myself *now* as severely as God will judge me at the moment of my death, I judge myself *in his stead*. I take his place momentarily to give time for my memory to tell me that *when* I am lying, from the reader's perspective my heart had to be innocent. This change of places between God and my inner conviction constitutes both the possibility of *innocent lies* and the necessity of the *reader's testimony*.

II. An Innocent Liar, a Truthful Man, and a Confessing Witness

A Lie Is a Fable

§ 1 Even if I do not harm anyone, no one could tell me if I am hurting myself. Yet, as we have seen, in order to be completely innocent, I must harm neither the other nor myself. But how can one be certain of this? At first glance it would suffice to consider one's own intentions and to ask oneself with the utmost sincerity if these intentions are free of deceit. Unfortunately, this is not a simple task because, for Rousseau, innocent lies are not a matter of good intentions: "But to make a lie innocent, it is not enough for there to be no deliberate intention to do harm; rather, it must be *certain* that the error into which one is throwing those to whom one is speaking cannot harm them or anyone else in any way whatsoever."[23] *Making* a lie innocent, or transforming it into erroneous speech that is free of harm, depends directly on this power of certainty. In other words, being certain that this error is harmless in a sense comes down to being sure of having judged one's own soul to the utmost degree. This means that one is certain of having seen *everything* and shown *everything*. This means that one has the innermost conviction that *when* I no longer see any harm within me, *when* my memory no longer brings any to mind, God himself will not see any. I must thus be convinced that my own judgment will not have anything to *expect* from the judgment of God. And as here I have told myself the truth, *all* the truth, I will not have any more secrets from God. There will be nothing left over, no debt, nothing to fear—my speech will have no effect, and all lies will become *fables*. As Rousseau writes: "To lie without benefit or harm to oneself or to others is not to lie: it is not a lie, but a fiction"—a moral fiction, a fable.[24]

We could say: *mendacium est fabula*, a lie is a fable. A lie is fabulous. But we must interpret this in the sense of Pindar's "sweet lie" and John Chrysostom's "well-timed deception."[25] The fabrication [*fabulation*] of a lie is a way of doing, acting, and thinking that consists in speaking so as to not say anything. This action belongs to "the person who tells a fable simply as a fable."[26] Thus, it is not a question of declaring something senseless but of stating that there is nothing left to say. In this type of discourse, the intention of the author is neither good nor bad but void or empty; it is a decision devoid of any "persuasion,"[27] address, or agreement. The intention no longer has an object, or, more precisely, it transforms its object into a narrative while making this narrative into the final degree of speech before asserting its own silence. Thus, we shift directly from a moral *intention* to a poetic *invention*.[28] A lie becomes a fable when the story that one invents allows one not to reduce one's speech to silence while producing in the heart of the other the same *effect* as silence. This is the meaning of the *rule*—the ability to maintain the narrative at the level of fiction. The fable would be so fictional and so pure (purer than a mute person's silence) that it would do away with all explicit references to its enunciation, to the point of effacing, or at least of disturbing, the authority of its own discourse. This is the quasi-silence of a discourse that only "disguises," surrounds, envelops the truth, embraces it without touching it, perhaps even without expressing it.[29] However, this discourse will *cost* me my life. If I cannot be certain of the fabrication of this narrative, how could I be convinced that there is no trace of deception left in my heart or any intention that God one day will have to *judge* at my expense and against my will? The salvation aspired for in the *Confessions* rests precisely on this question.

§ 2 Rousseau distinguishes between the truth of the man of the world and the truth of the *truthful* man. The first would always speak *about* the world, listing names, places, and dates, remaining loyal to sources in a discourse of flawless precision. But in matters of intimate concern and relating directly to his or her life, this person would speak only in a self-serving way. By contrast, vehemently mocking such truths, the *truthful* man would acknowledge responsibility for acts and texts to the point of risking his life, certain of never having said anything less than the entire truth about his life. As Rousseau writes: "The difference, then, between my truthful man and the other is that the man of the world is rigorously faithful to any truth which does not cost him anything, but no more than that, whereas my man never serves truth so faithfully as when he has to *lay down his life* for its sake."[30] This is the Abbé Rozier's maxim: *vitam vero impendenti*. The life of a *truthful* man comes at a price, and it is this price that must be destroyed, sacrificed, exchanged, spent. One must dedicate one's life to telling the truth, beyond all truth and all value of truth. This self-sacrifice, or the sacrifice of one's subjectivity, this relinquishment of authority, is a critical concept but one that is difficult to define. It is an economy that consists in exchanging one's life for a feeling of certainty—the conviction of having said *all* the truth.

In order to understand what is at stake in such a sacrifice, let us be as concrete as Rousseau and return to the example of the lie made about "poor Marion." Thus, let us turn once again to the *Confessions*. The narration of this event occurs in three stages: (1) The scene of the stolen ribbon. It is very brief and its sole purpose is to describe the desire *to steal for the sake of stealing*. "I was tempted only by this ribbon, I stole it."[31] (2) Hardly interested in possessing this ribbon, he did not think of hiding it. Thus, left visible, this ribbon was very quickly discovered and Rousseau was asked to justify himself. This leads to the *embarrassment* and the *accusation of an innocent person*: "I hesitated, stammered, and finally said, blushing, that Marion had given it to me."[32] (3) What follows is the moment of *obstinacy*, a *refusal to confess* (publicly) to his "crime" despite the tears of the innocent girl: "I persisted in my infernal wickedness, however, repeated my accusation, and asserted to her face that it was she who had given me the ribbon."[33] A line of reasoning corresponds to each of these moments. The desire to possess is justified by the fact that the satisfaction of a desire is natural and that the fruits of the earth do not belong to anyone.[34] The refusal to confess is justified by the feeling of false shame, humiliation, and wounded self-love.[35] The intermediary scene, the moment of embarrassment, proves more difficult to justify. It is a pure irruption of lies. Impetuous and overwhelming, this act lasts only an instant, but an instant that is contradictory or paradoxical. The emergence of a lie is situated between the *worst* and *nothing*, between a nameless crime and a decision without immediate remorse. This is how Rousseau attempts to explain this paradox.

§ 3 According to the Fourth Walk, this lie would only have been "a product of false shame," like a moment of madness in which "my innate timidity got the better of all the wishes of my heart."[36] In the *Confessions*, however, this explanation is more nuanced, and the paradoxical causes of this lie are clearly distinguished, if not problematized. I would even go so far as to say that the purpose of the *Confessions* depends directly on this explanation. The faithful account of this scene of the stolen ribbon and the belated confession of the lie no longer suffice, for a justification is necessary as well. "But I would not be fulfilling the *purpose of this book* if I did not at the same time reveal my own innermost feelings, and if I were afraid to excuse myself, even where the truth of the matter calls for it."[37] As I have just shown, after the scene of theft Rousseau speaks about two different moments in time, distinguished by two types of inner dispositions (embarrassment and *then* false shame). The fact that the Fourth Walk does not take such a difference into account is very significant. In trying to authenticate, in vain, the validity of the confessed truths, and in providing a psychological reason (false shame, self-love, etc.) to explain and justify the cause of the lie, this confession of the *Confessions* in a sense had to extract the *paradox* of his innocence from the lie, and thus to reproduce the internal structure of a lie through a kind of overlap of two texts. This confession dissimulates the troubling fact that the transformation of the lie into fiction is not the result of the author's pure innocence but rather that of the radical unworking of the reader to whom the narrative of such a lie is addressed. However, in the *Confessions* these two moments involve two different dispositions. The first one is pure embarrassment, whose internal conflict is precisely what constitutes the "possibility of such a lie. The second one, which immediately follows this conflict, emerges from yet another conflict: between the harm inflicted on the innocent girl and the presence of so many people who demand from her a justification.[38] This latter conflict produces shame and humiliation, and it is at this moment that Rousseau blindly and obstinately denies his crime.

The false shame is thus not the *cause* of the lie; it represents instead its most immediate *effect*. But in that case, under what conditions can a heart so pure be capable of producing a lie? Let us turn to Rousseau's own explanation:

> I have never been less motivated by malice than at this *cruel moment*, and when I accused this unfortunate girl, it is bizarre, but it is true, that it was my *fondness* for her that was the cause of it. She was on my mind, and I had simply used as an excuse the first object that presented itself to me. I accused her of having done what I wanted to do, and of having given me the ribbon, because my intention had been to give it to her.[39]

This text contains a vicious cycle.[40] It is a kind of machination that defines the paradoxical moment of the lie, between the cruelty of a moment and the purity of feelings. At this moment, both pure and cruel, an act would then take shape, the cause or the reason for which was fondness, *[amitié]* as Rousseau claims. Following Rousseau's reasoning, I address my act not only *to* the one I love—to Marion, an irresistible young girl, so sweet and pretty—but, more importantly, I address her *because at this moment* she is the one I love.[41] Yet, this act must not be considered as a "crime of passion caused by love." This affair is less sentimental than it might seem. Rather, it is a quasi-automatic strategy, a mechanical transfer of causes between "I accuse myself" (*ex-causa*) and "I accuse" (*ad-causa*): a kind of *back and forth* of the cause, which is immediately associated with the reciprocal change of places (between the one who steals and the one who gives), the symmetrical confusion of exchange (between stealing and giving), and the systematic inversion of authority figures (between the author of the narrative and the reader).

Due to the simple fact that his fondness for Marion was present in his mind when he wanted to give her this stolen ribbon, this theft transforms into a gift from Marion. Rousseau does not say that Marion *stole* the ribbon but that she *gave* it to him—in other words that she did exactly what he wanted to do. Therefore, she is not accused of stealing but of giving.[42] In addition, by accusing her of doing not what he himself did but what he wanted to do, thus giving him what he himself had stolen, Rousseau transforms this imaginary and love-driven gift into an *effacement* of his theft, one that is indeed real.[43] However, by taking Marion as the object of his excuse, by using her *as* an excuse, he does not accuse her yet in the strict sense of the term. Between these two moments of the cause, there is a distinction that must be carefully explained.

The *Confessions* provides a way to apologize without an excuse, without apologizing, or, to be more precise, without taking the excuse for a motive that allows the one who confesses to excuse oneself or to substitute one's cause with an exculpation or a purely fictional act. If the excuse had been the only reason for this substitution, by using Marion as an excuse, Rousseau would have simply accused her, nothing more and nothing less. And by apologizing, he would not really have excused himself but instead accused himself; he would have simply admitted to the depravity of his crime and recognized the authority of his act (his guilt as his ultimate identity). For one to be able to infer from his excuses that he is accusing himself and that he therefore recognizes his guilt or sees himself as the *subject* of guilt, he must not, in using Marion as an excuse, accuse her in any way. In order to avoid entering the tragic cycle (he who excuses himself accuses himself; he who accuses himself excuses himself), one must distinguish between two levels or types of excuses. The first concerns the ultimate goal of the *Confessions*: "to tell all the truth." In order for this book's goal to be achieved, I must not be "afraid to *excuse myself*," writes Rousseau. In other words, as I was completely innocent at that moment, I must not be afraid to accuse myself by excusing myself of this lie: "I have never been less motivated by malice than at this cruel moment." In this case the excuse consists in revealing the confessed truths in their entirety and thus reducing the reader's interpretation to a reading that is partial and inadequate but also biased, tendentious, and dishonest.[44] And it is in the narrative of this excuse that another excuse is produced, an excuse *for* the excuse *in* the excuse. It is an excuse that would try to prevent the great excuse of the *Confessions* (one on which it is founded) from being interpreted in a partial or biased manner and thus from being expressed as an accusation. "She [Marion] was on my mind, and I had simply *used as an excuse* the first object that presented itself to me." For Rousseau, it is no longer a question of apologizing, of explaining himself in order to absolve himself of a wrongdoing and to dispense justice on his own behalf, but rather of effacing his position as author or subject. By saying *I used as an* excuse, *I effaced myself at* "the first object that presented itself to me." I effaced all causes, all explicit references, all possible places of accusation, and thus all legitimate authority from the place from which I speak and excuse myself. Between the fondness for Marion in my mind and the moment when she becomes guilty, there is nothing, and it is not my fault. There is only an "object" by which *I am no longer present at the place where my excuse accuses me.* This is the reason for the possible and at the same time necessary confusion between Rousseau's theft and Marion's gift.

By effacing the first excuse from questioning or any real accusation, the second excuse would have nullified any possible relation of reference between the order of discourse and the order of things and thus any possible form of presupposed authority, presumed responsibility, and guilt. There would be no accusation without an accuser, an absolute authority, or at least without a direct, real, and intentional link between the one who excuses himself and the one who accuses himself. Therefore, if the act of excusing oneself no longer necessarily implies that one accuses oneself, by excusing oneself the one who confesses would no longer accuse oneself of accusing an innocent person. One must now *take the other's place*, deprive them of it, in order to accuse them of such an accusation. For when Rousseau excuses himself by stating that "Marion had given it to me," he does not directly accuse the young girl of stealing the ribbon but rather erases the difference between the reality of the actual theft and his desire to give a gift. It is precisely because Marion did *in his stead* what he had wanted to do, in other words transform his theft into a gift, that there is no difference for Rousseau between saying "I stole" and "she had given it to me." Thus, his own theft transforms into the other's act of giving, and his lie becomes *innocent.* Marion understood perfectly the ambiguity of her misfortune. Her serene reply is proof of this: "How wretched you are making me, and yet *I would not for anything be in your place.*"[45] This place, however, is neither entirely Marion's nor truly Rousseau's but rather that of an interchangeable object, through which the figure of Marion can *represent* the future innocence of Rousseau's lie. "Marion's gift" could also be described as a purely fictional object, an object without direct reference or facticity, whose *narrative* confounds the reality of a theft with the moment of a desire. And it is this confusion that will give rise to the problematic figure of the reader.[46] The difficulty then lies in maintaining this object, or this excuse, within the realm of fiction. In other words this object would need to be constructed as the narrative of a purely fictional and inoffensive "event," a kind of spontaneous, automatic, or mechanical process, like a diabolical machine of a fabulous innocence. In this case, however, where does the cruelty of this act come from, if this act is not cruel in itself? This is the paradox of an innocent lie. Once this act is performed and formulated, the internal confusion between "I excuse myself" and "I accuse" is judged, interpreted, lost in the world, and my own confessions accuse me by the simple fact that my excuses transform, at my own expense, into an accusation of Marion. I am identified as the subject of my actions whereby I become guilty. I am *now* accused of being the author of a crime, of lying and denouncing an innocent girl, even though I did nothing more than tell the truth. In regarding my action as a lie, it is the reader's interpretation that transforms me into an author. My lie is the product of the reader's *work*; my authority depends on them; my identity is their judgment. The reader is the one who *retroactively* establishes the connections between facts, between a discourse and a reality, between a book and a life. The reader not only creates connections that have never existed *at the moment* that I make excuses but also transforms me into the accused and identifies me as the guilty one, even though these connections have never existed within me nor for me. The figure of this reader is very problematic; it must be examined, and the reader's interpretation, judgment, confession, and risk of false testimony must be questioned.

Sacrifice: Telling All the Truth

§ 1 "It is for the reader to assemble all these elements and to determine the be-ing that they constitute; the result must be his own *work*, so that if he is mis-taken, all the error is on his side. . . . It is not for me to judge the importance of the facts; I must simply say everything and leave to him the task of choosing among them."[47] This reader is a true demiurge, a divine architect who is capable of assembling elements so as to compose a being in its singularity. When the reader *reads, at every instant* of reading, he or she *produces* a new composition, consisting not only of recited or narrated elements but also of these narrations and facts.[48] The reader selects, sorts, classifies, and at the same time produces, identifying subjects, considering facts, and deciding on the meaning of the narrative.[49] Just as to think is to judge for the Savoyard vicar, here "to read is to decide, to produce," and thus to form the identity of an author.[50] Rousseau may have indeed confessed, but the *Confessions* is nonetheless the *work* of the reader. It becomes difficult to distinguish between Rousseau's confessions and the "confessions" of the reader, all the more so because in portraying himself Rousseau makes the reader confess.[51] Indeed, how can we read the discourse of the person who confesses without considering it as the work of the *Confes-sions*—without attributing to it an author or a subject who is identified as being responsible for it, and thus in this sense without interpreting the dismissal of his excuse as implicit proof of his own accusation?

For Rousseau, to confess is to say *all* the truth, *nothing* but the truth. But who could ever claim to have been able to read the entirety of a confessed truth? When Rousseau will have said everything or promised to say everything, to show and to reveal everything, when he comes before God without giving him the slightest chance to judge him, what meaning could the reader's judgment still have? Faced with "saying everything" of the one who confesses, the reader has only one possi-bility: to read as one would read any other book—to interpret, evaluate, and then judge. In this case, however, the reader will not have heard the "entirety" of the confessed truths. He will make this discourse his own work, and this narrative will become his own "confessions," no more, no less. When the reader judges and interprets—for this is how he produces a work—his reading will need to be con-sidered as partial, interested, and thus erroneous and misleading. This reading will not be accused of interpreting *wrongly* but of *interpreting*—as if the act itself of interpreting, reading, or even thinking had in principle always already been derived from a desire to do harm, to mislead, and especially to seek revenge.[52] Another "type" of reading can be used here, a kind of reading that would consist in not reading what is read, a reading whose "act of reading" would have the power to confuse that which is "read"—"that which is confessed" in the uttered discourse—with the "illegibility" of the confessions, "that which exceeds" or "that which resists" all judgment, all interpretation, all production of works, and thus all identification of authority. This is a kind of reading that would no longer have the function of overcoming or resolving the author's internal imbalance, the loss of his identity, of his guilt, and of being put to death, nor of mourning this loss, of preventing this loss by effacing it through a hermeneutic reconstruction, a sense, a meaning, a reason. However, the undertaking of this reading will be purely testimonial, like an infinite work of memory. And this is how we will shift from the reader's *interpretation* to the reader's *testimony*.

Rousseau now addresses the witness-reader in the following terms:

> But the undertaking I have embarked on, to reveal myself to him in my entirety, requires that nothing about me should remain hidden or obscure; I must be continually present to his gaze; he must follow me into all the aberrations of my heart, into every recess of my life; *he must not lose sight of me for a moment*, for fear that, finding in my story the least lacuna, the least void, and wondering to himself what I did during that time, he should accuse me of not wanting to reveal everything.[53]

Saying the truth in its entirety, or confessing, thus comes down to no longer leaving time for the reader's reading. There would no longer be any void or place to put this reading in a *position* to judge. Every instant, every second, every heartbeat of the one who confesses would be revealed, cited, and recounted. The reader will no longer be in a position to interpret any part of the narrative that has not yet been openly stated. Now, it is the *eye* of the reader that will be absent. It is this accusatory eye, the interpreter of lies, this vengeful eye, the fabricator of lies, that Rousseau inevitably had to appropriate: "I had necessarily to say how, *if I were someone else*, I would view a man such as myself."[54] Rousseau deprives the reader of his eye, not by destroying it with his admissions but by blinding the reader with his suspended and absolute presence: "I must be continually present to his gaze [*ses yeux*]." For the reader, to see everything continually is to no longer see at all. And if there is no more time to see and to judge, to read and to interpret, this is because his own reading always comes too late. It comes *after* this moment of the infallible verdict, in which the judgment of God is anticipated. Yet can one truly judge the Last Judgment? Can one read and interpret it without destroying or discrediting it? And above all, can one transform it into a literary work?

§ 2 The reader had to be blinded, unworked [*désœuvré*], and mourned for his reading to become that of a witness rather than that of an interpreter. This other kind of reading, this reading of the illegible, one that is purely testimonial, consists in interpreting, in the confessed discourse, the *sacrifice* of a life and of authority rather than the *narrative* of a life, with its moments of joy, suffering, errors, and desires. As we have already noted, according to Rousseau to confess is to devote one's life to truth and thus to sacrifice oneself *for* truth. And this sacrifice requires a very specific economy. When confessing, I *give* myself to be interpreted entirely, unaltered, openly, and totally, to the point of death. I give myself when, before God, I am at my most vulnerable, where my authority is exposed and without secrets, at a point in my discourse where, being absolutely naked, I have at once *the most* to fear and *nothing* to fear.[55] It is here, at this moment of giving fully and relentlessly, that my narrative becomes illegible, that the biased gaze of the reader is reduced to that of a witness, and that my innocence is commemorated as infinite mourning and as the last admission of this reading.

During the paradoxical moment of the innocent lie, the witness as reader becomes the guarantor of this exchange. By using his reading as an act of sacrifice rather than as the meaning of a narrative and consequently by admitting that faced with this offering he is no longer in a position to be the author of his reading and thus to give authority to the confessed discourse—or to accuse it of apologizing—, this reader admits *to himself* that he has produced the grieving memory of innocence as an admission. Indeed, if the reader admits to himself that what he reads can have no other effect on him but silence, the silence of God to the utterance of the *Confessions*, this discourse will remain at the level of fiction and all lies will become innocent. The reader will not need to prove anything to anyone—to the author, to another reader, or to God. Instead, he will himself represent the figure of the ultimate reader, as a purely gracious, generous, and sublime witness. He will become this blind, deaf, and mute witness, who admits to himself that at the place and the time that the sacrificed life of the one who confesses commits his heart only to the silence of the Last Judgment, his reading will have produced nothing more than the admission of a fabulous innocence, both necessary and impossible. As I have already pointed out, his admission of being an impostor to the sovereign's authority is necessary, while remaining for the reader an impossible act of reading. This imposture is not a deliberate intention of reading but rather an act that forms the status of the reader or his position as interpreter. This is the *unworking* effect of the paradox proper to all innocent lies.

Either the reader becomes the witness of his own admission of innocence (and this is what I would call a pure witness of grace, an unworked witness, stripped of his authority as interpreter), or he is himself treated as a liar whose reading would thereby be accused of false testimony. In the last pages of the *Confessions*, Rousseau writes: "I have told the truth. If anyone knows things that are contrary to what I have just set out, should they be proved a thousand times over, he knows lies and deceits . . . [it is this man who] ought to be stifled."[56] This constitutes a symbolic killing of the reader, their exposure as an impostor. The reader's authority as interpreter is now compared to the vindictive figure of a liar. Just as the identity of the "author" of the *Confessions* could not be reduced to the juridical identity of a guilty person, the hermeneutic identity of the reader could no longer protect the meaning of his reading from the desire for imposture, slander, and lies. However, the unworking or the internal instability of the reader does not reduce all interpretations to insignificance but rather transforms them into testimony. This is the testimony of his own unworking, like an admission that is made before the sovereign silence of the paradox of an innocent discourse. God's silence to what is said at every instant makes the discourse *illegible* and the literary work impossible. Such is the case not in the sense that God alone has the power of interpretation but rather in the sense that God will himself have always already exercised his power. Ultimately, this is what the reader's testimony must reveal: a kind of anticipation that is indistinguishable from the irreducible delay in his or her interpretation. The reader is expected to admit this delay while at the same time admitting in advance that God's judgment will have always already taken place. This is the reason for the reader's irreducible unworking and the infinite scope of his mourning. He needs to bear witness to this not *to* God but *for* God. The reader witnesses *in his place* that everything he has read has been confessed, as God himself will have always already seen it. This paradoxical moment of silence lasts only the time that is necessary for one to come before God as God, to be like him before him, and to ask him for the worst: to gather all of his witnesses-readers around this book in order for them to admit *in his place* that his own silence is the indisputable proof that there has never been nor will there ever be innocence so untarnished, so perfect, and so pure.

> I am resolved on an undertaking that has no model and will have no imitator. I want to show my fellow-men a man in all the truth of nature; and this man is to be myself.
>
> Myself alone. I feel my heart and I know men. I am not made like any that I have seen; I venture to believe that I was not made like any that exist. If I am not more deserving, at least I am different. As to whether nature did well or ill to break the mould in which I was cast, that is something no one can judge until after they have read me.
>
> Let the trumpet of judgement sound when it will, I will present myself with this book in my hand before the Supreme Judge. I will say boldly: "Here is what I have done, what I have thought, what I was. I have told the good and the bad with equal frankness. I have concealed nothing that was ill, added nothing that was good, and if I have sometimes used some indifferent ornamentation,

this has only ever been to fill a void occasioned by my lack of memory; I may have supposed to be true what I knew could have been so, never what I knew to be false. I have shown myself as I was, contemptible and vile when that is how I was, good, generous, sublime, when that is how I was; I have disclosed my innermost self as you alone know it to be. Assemble about me, Eternal Being, the numberless host of my fellow-men; let them hear my confessions, let them groan at my unworthiness, let them blush at my wretchedness. Let each of them, here on the steps of your throne, in turn reveal his heart with the same sincerity; and then let one of them say to you, if he dares: *I was better than that man.*[57]

Notes

Presented in 1994 in Jacques Derrida's seminar at the École des hautes études en sciences sociales, this text was first published in the *Archives de philosophie* no. 63 (2000).

1. The act of questioning the critical neutrality of reading is already a way of stripping the reader of hermeneutic authority. As we will see, this transforms every reader into a liar. What Roland Barthes referred to at the end of the 1960s as "the death of the author" (the irreducible difference between the author's life and his or her work) for Rousseau required the putting to death or the hermeneutic deposition of the reader (the indissoluble link between the free will of the reader's interpretation and his or her biased reading or desire for revenge). Cf. Barthes, "The Death of the Author," in *Image, Music, Text*, trans. S. Heath (London: Fontana, 1977), esp. 147.

2. On this subject see the remarkable analyses by Peggy Kamuf, *Signature Pieces: On the Institution of Authorship* (Ithaca, NY: Cornell University Press, 1988), and Geoffrey Bennington, *Dudding: Des noms de Rousseau* (Paris: Galilée, 1991).

3. Cf. Jean Starobinski, *Jean-Jacques Rousseau: La transparence et l'obstacle* (Paris: Gallimard, 1970), 226; *Rousseau: Transparency and Obstruction*, trans. Arthur Goldhammer (Chicago: University of Chicago Press, 1988).

4. The scene of the stolen ribbon appears at the end of book 2 of the *Confessions,* trans. Angela Scholar (Oxford: Oxford University Press, 2000), 82–85. For the Fourth Walk, see Rousseau, *Reveries of the Solitary Walker*, trans. Russell Goulbourne (Oxford: Oxford University Press, 2011), 33–48. Paul de Man deals essentially with the scene of the stolen ribbon in "Excuses (Confessions)," in *Allegories of Reading* (New Haven, CT: Yale University Press, 1979), 278–279, a key text to which I will return. Jacques Derrida analyzes it in "Typewriter Ribbon: Limited Ink (2)," in *Without Alibi*, ed., trans., and with an introduction by Peggy Kamuf (Stanford: Stanford University Press, 2002), 71–160.

5. Rousseau, *Confessions*, 3, emphasis added. [Translation modified.—Trans.]

6. In the "Profession of Faith of the Savoyard Vicar," in *Emile*, the "good testimony of oneself" is associated with the most sublime state of happiness. It does not suffice for the mind to be free, for it must also be used properly. "He would be happy, it is true. But his happiness would be lacking the most sublime degree, the glory of virtue and the good witness of oneself." Rousseau, *Emile, or On Education*, vol. 13 of *The Collected Writings of Rousseau*, ed. Christopher Kelly, trans. Allan Bloom and Christopher Kelly (Hanover, NH: University Press of New England, 2010), 456. See also ibid., 481, and Rousseau, *My Portrait*, vol. 12 of *The*

Collected Writings of Rousseau, trans. and ed. Christopher Kelly (Hanover, NH: University Press of New England, 2007), (17), 39.

7. Rousseau, *Confessions*, 82.

8. Ibid., 84.

9. Rousseau, *Reveries*, Fourth Walk, 34, emphasis added. "What surprised me most was that, as I recalled these invented things, I felt no real remorse for them. I, whose horror of falsehood is completely unmatched in my heart by anything else and who would willingly endure torture if the alternative was to avoid it by lying, by what bizarre inconsistency could I thus lie so cheerfully, unnecessarily, and pointlessly, and by what inconceivable contradiction could I do so without feeling the slightest regret, when remorse for a lie has continually afflicted me for fifty years?"

10. Ibid.

11. Ibid. [Translation modified.—Trans.]

12. From Plato to Sartre, a certain notion of lying is founded on the idea that all forms of deception necessarily involve a minimum of knowledge. See Plato, *Lesser Hippias*, in *Cratilus; Parmenides; Greater Hippias; Lesser Hippias*, trans. Harold North Fowler, Loeb Classical Library 167 (Cambridge, MA: Harvard University Press, 1926), 367a, 367e, 369b, 370e, 372a, and 376a; Plato, *Republic, Books 1–5*, ed. and trans. Christopher Emlyn-Jones and William Preddy, Loeb Classical Library 237 (Cambridge, MA: Harvard University Press, 2013), 382b–c, and Jean-Paul Sartre, *Being and Nothingness*, trans. and with an introduction by Hazel E. Barnes (New York: Washington Square Press, 1992), esp. 87. As in the case of the "noble lie" in Plato's *Republic* III, 414a–415d—see also Plato, *Statesman*, in *Statesman; Philebus; Ion*, trans. Harold North Fowler and W. R. M. Lamb, Loeb Classical Library 164 (Cambridge, MA: Harvard University Press, 1925), 304c–d, and *Laws, Books 1–6*, trans. R. G. Bury, Loeb Classical Library 187 (Cambridge, MA: Harvard University Press, 1926), II, 663d–664b—the legislator of the social contract will also need to resort to the "sacred lie" of persuasion in order to create laws: "The legislator therefore, being unable to appeal to either force or reason, must have recourse to an authority of a different order, capable of constraining without violence and persuading without convincing. This is what has, in all ages, compelled the fathers of nations to have recourse to divine intervention and credit the gods with their own wisdom, in order that the peoples, submitting to the laws of the State as to those of nature, and recognizing the same power in the formation of the city as in that of man, might obey freely, and bear with docility the yoke of the public happiness." Rousseau, *Social Contract*, vol. 4 of *The Collected Writings of Rousseau*, ed. Roger D. Masters and Christopher Kelly; trans. Judith R. Bush, Roger D. Masters, and Christopher Kelly (Hanover, NH: University Press of New England, 1994), 216. See Bennington, *Dudding: Des noms de Rousseau*, 75, n. 1. The Kantian imperative rejects any deviation from the "sacred" law of truthfulness. Cf. Immanuel Kant, *Grounding for the Metaphysics of Morals: On a Supposed Right to Lie Because of Philanthropic Concerns* (1797), trans. James W. Ellington (Indianapolis, IN: Hackett, 1993), esp. 68.

13. Rousseau, *Reveries*, Fourth Walk, 35.

14. Ibid., 36. See also Rousseau, *Dialogues: On the Subject and Form of This Writing*, vol. 1 of *The Collected Writings of Rousseau*, ed. Roger D. Masters and Christopher Kelly; trans. Judith R. Bush, Roger D. Masters, and Christopher Kelly (Hanover, NH: University Press of New England, 1990), 166.

15. Ibid.

16. Augustine, *Lying*, in *Saint Augustine: Treatises on Various Subjects*, trans. Mary Sarah Muldowney, ed. Roy Deferrari (Washington, DC: Catholic University of America Press,

2002), (17), 77–78. Saint Augustine links the question of lying directly to the enigma of martyrdom as the absolute refusal to give false testimony. Must one renounce one's faith (one's soul) in order to save one's life (one's body) (cf. ibid., section VI)? In their correspondence, Saint Augustine and Saint Jerome discuss Saint Paul's supposed lie (for more on this subject see Michèle Sinapi, "Le mensonge officieux dans la correspondance Jérôme-Augustin," *Rue Descartes* 8–9 [1993]: 63–83). Just like Saint Peter, the leader of the Apostles, Saint Paul, the leader of the Pagans, considered the adherence to the Judaic practice of circumcision useless for the salvation of the soul (Acts 15:1–7 and 21:21). Nevertheless, giving into the pressure by converted Jews, he himself circumcised several of his friends (Timothy and Jude) (Acts 16:3). Did he lie or give false testimony about the dogma of the New Covenant? What is then the relation between circumcision, lying, and false testimony? In short, how does one shift from the Old Covenant to the New Covenant without lying? To put it differently, how can one transform circumcision into uncircumcision? "Now, how can one reattach foreskin that has been cut off?" (*Quomodo enim potest adduci praeputium quod praecisum est*; *Lying* [8], 63). [English translation modified by E. Yampolsky in reference to Serge Margel's modification of the French translation.—Trans.] In other words, how can the New Covenant be founded by putting the foreskin back in its place, so to speak? In reference to prophet Jeremiah's discourse on the circumcision of the heart (Jer. 4:4; cf. Deut. 30:6), as described by Saint Paul in Rom, 2:29, Hilary of Poitiers had already summed up, several decades before the beginning of this correspondence, the high stakes of the debate: "As one [Joshua] comes after Moses, the other comes after the Law. As one received the order to renew circumcision with a stone knife, the Lord (*ita a Domino*), who is the sharp verb that penetrates to the point of division of the soul and the angular stone, spiritually inaugurated the circumcision of the heart." Hilary of Poitiers, *Traité des mystères* (*Tractatus mysteriorum*), ed. and trans. J.-P. Brisson (Paris: Le Cerf, 1947), II, ch. 6, 151. [Quotation translated by E. Yampolsky.—Trans.]

17. Rousseau, *Reveries*, Fourth Walk, 36. And this is precisely why a lie cannot corrupt, hurt, or alter the resources of innocence and truth. Cf. Rousseau, *Notes for the Reveries*, vol. 12 of *The Collected Writings of Rousseau*, trans. and ed. Christopher Kelly (Hanover, NH: University Press of New England, 2007), (29), 56, and Rousseau, *Biographical Fragment*, vol. 12 of *The Collected Writings of Rousseau*, trans. and ed. Christopher Kelly (Hanover, NH: University Press of New England, 2007), 31. In addition, a silent, innocent lie constitutes a true principle or law of education. "From these reflections I draw the solution to the question so often debated—whether it is fitting to enlighten children early concerning the objects of their curiosity, or whether it is better to put them off the train with little falsehoods? I think one ought to do neither the one nor the other. In the first place, this curiosity does not come to them without someone's having provided the occasion for it. One must therefore act in such a way that they do not have such curiosity. In the second place, questions one is not forced to answer do not require deceiving the child who asks them. It is better to impose silence on him than to answer him by lying. He will be little surprised by this law if care has been taken to subject him to it in inconsequential things" (Rousseau, *Emile*, 367). Considering that a child has not yet developed a relation to the law, the disengagement of the child's speech cannot be defined in terms of a broken promise. Therefore, it is not relevant to speak about a child's lies. "Since a child does not know what he is doing when he commits himself, then he cannot lie in committing himself. It is not the same when he breaks his promise, which is now a kind of retroactive lie, for he remembers very well having made this promise; but what he does not see is the importance of keeping it. Not in a condition to read the future, he cannot foresee the consequences of things, and when he violates his commitments, he does nothing contrary to the reason of his age. It

follows from this that children's lies are all the work of masters, and that to want to teach them to tell the truth is nothing other than to teach them to lie" (Rousseau, *Emile*, 236; see also ibid., 235). The shift from the child's innocent lie to the acquisition of well-reasoned lies ultimately finds its origin in the violence of the question. Such is the case when I ask the child: "Was it you?" (ibid., 237). "Nothing is more indiscreet than such a question, especially when the child is guilty: then if he believes that you know that he did it, he will see that you are setting a trap for him, and this opinion cannot fail to turn him against you. If he does not believe it, he will say to himself, 'Why should I reveal my offense?' And this is the first temptation to lie, the effect of your imprudent question" (ibid., 237); see note. As Rousseau sees it, the question of gender difference must also be taken into account with regard to lying: He believes a masculine lie is expressed with speech and the mouth, whereas a feminine lie manifests itself in the materiality of the voice, the accent, the breath, or the respiration: "We are told that women are false. They become so. Their particular gift is skill and not falseness. According to the true inclinations of their sex, even when they are lying they are not false. Why do you consult their mouth when it is not the mouth which ought to speak? Consult their eyes, their color, their breathing, their fearful manner, their soft resistance. This is the language nature gives them for answering you. The mouth always says no and ought to say so. But the accent it adds to this answer is not always the same, and this accent does not know how to lie. Does not woman have the same needs as man without having the same right to express them?" (ibid., 563).

18. Rousseau, *Reveries*, Fourth Walk, 37.

19. Ibid., 37 and 41–42.

20. "In continuing to follow my method, I do not draw these rules from the principles of a high philosophy, but find them written by nature with ineffaceable characters in the depth of my heart" ("Profession of Faith of the Savoyard Vicar," in Rousseau, *Emile*, 448). See also Rousseau, *Reveries*, Third Walk, 27.

21. Rousseau, *Reveries*, Fourth Walk, 37.

22. Ibid. "But far from having passed over or concealed anything that could be used in evidence against me, by a turn of mind which I struggle to understand and which perhaps derives from my antipathy towards all kinds of imitation, I felt more inclined to lie in the opposite way, by accusing myself too severely rather than by excusing myself too indulgently, and my conscience assures me that one day I shall be judged less severely than I judge myself" (ibid., 44). The same idea appears in the *Dialogues*: "The hope that these *Confessions* would not be seen until after his death gave him the courage to say everything, and to treat himself with a justice that is often even too rigorous" (Rousseau, *Dialogues*, 188).

23. Rousseau, *Reveries*, Fourth Walk, 38, emphasis added.

24. Ibid.

25. Pindar, *Nemean*, in *Nemean Odes; Isthmian Odes; Fragments*, ed. and trans. William H. Race, Loeb Classical Library 485 (Cambridge, MA: Harvard University Press, 1997), 7, 23–24. [See Pindar, *Pythians*, in *Olympian Odes; Pythian Odes*, trans. and ed. William H. Race, Loeb Classical Library 56 (Cambridge, MA: Harvard University Press, 1997), 2, 37.—Trans.] John Chrysostom, *On the Priesthood*, trans. W. R. W. Stephens, in Select Library of Nicene and Post Nicene Fathers, ser. 1, vol. 9, ed. Ph. Schaff (London: T. & T. Clark, 1889), bk. 1, 8, 37.

26. Rousseau, *Reveries*, Fourth Walk, 38.

27. Ibid., 39.

28. "Stripped of all moral usefulness, the true value of these [fictions] can only be judged in terms of the intention of the person who invents them, and when he tells them in earnest, as if they were really true, it is hard to disagree that they are really lies" (ibid., 38).

29. Ibid.

30. Ibid., 40. Cf. Rousseau, *Notes for the Reveries* (18), 54.

31. Rousseau, *Confessions*, bk. 2, 82.

32. Ibid.

33. Ibid., 83.

34. This idea is already present in the second *Discourse*: "you are lost if you forget that the fruits belong to all and the Earth to no one" (Rousseau, *Discourse on the Origin*, 43).

35. "It was not that I was afraid of being punished but that I was afraid of being put to shame; and I feared shame more than death, more than crime, more than anything in the world. I would have wanted the earth to swallow me up and bury me in its depths. It was shame alone, unconquerable shame, that prevailed over everything and was the cause of all my imprudence; and the more criminal I became, the more my terror at having to admit it made me bold. All I could think of was the horror of being found out and of being denounced, publicly and to my face, as a thief, a liar, a slanderer. The confusion that seized my whole being robbed me of any other feeling" (Rousseau, *Confessions*, 84–85). See also Rousseau, *Reveries*, Fourth Walk, 43, and ibid., Sixth Walk, 62, as well as Rousseau, *Dialogues*, 184. On the relation between lying, shame, and the public space, see André Charrak, "Le récit de Rousseau comme épreuve de la liberté de conscience," *Revue de synthèse* 3–4 ["Autobiographies et courants spirituels"] (1996): 430–431.

36. Rousseau, *Reveries*, Fourth Walk, 33 and 34.

37. Rousseau, *Confessions*, bk. 2, 84, emphasis added. In this sentence and its context, Paul de Man distinguishes between two levels of reference: that of the confession strictly speaking, which is stated as a factual truth and the proof of which is referential in the strict sense (the theft of the ribbon and its discovery), and that of the excuse stated as truth in the confessions, the evidence of which will need to remain verbal (De Man, *Allegories of Reading*, 280). We can verify a confession but not an excuse. Thus, de Man establishes a very complex system of substitution between the confession of the repressed desire for Marion (represented by the stolen ribbon) and shame as an excuse: "shame used as an excuse permits repression to function as revelation and thus to make pleasure and guilt interchangeable. Guilt is forgiven because it allows for the pleasure of revealing its repression. It follows that repression is in fact an excuse, one speech act among others" (ibid., 286 and 288–289).

38. The temporal gap is manifest. "When she [Marion] appeared shortly afterwards I was stricken with remorse, but the presence of so many people was stronger than my repentance" (Rousseau, *Confessions*, 84).

39. Ibid., emphasis added.

40. The notion of machination appears often in the Fourth Walk: "So it is clear that neither my judgement nor my will dictated my response and that it was the automatic effect of my embarrassment" (Rousseau, *Reveries*, Fourth Walk, 44). See also ibid., Sixth Walk, 59. [In reference to Rousseau's term *machinal*, Margel uses the French word *machination*, which refers both to automatism and to the English term "machination," as in a plot or conspiracy.—Trans.]

41. "Not only was Marion pretty, she also had a freshness of complexion that is found only in the mountains, and, above all, an air of modesty and sweetness that won the heart of everyone who saw her" (Rousseau, *Confessions*, 82). [Translation modified.—Trans.]

42. Marion's gift is forced only because she is accused of giving it, and it is precisely because this gift is forced, imposed, or obliged that it can be defined as a theft. "Now, any gift made by force is not a gift, it is a theft" (Rousseau, *Dialogues*, 67). Even though it is he who

imposed it on her, the difficulty for Rousseau lies in receiving this forced gift: "Of whatever value a present offered might be and whatever it costs the one who is offering it, since it costs me even more to accept it, the one from whom it comes is indebted to me" (Rousseau, *My Portrait* [29], 41; cf. Rousseau, *Letters to Malesherbes*, vol. 5 of *The Collected Writings of Rousseau*, ed. Christopher Kelly, Roger D. Masters, and Peter G. Stillman; trans. Christopher Kelly [Hanover, NH: University Press of New England, 1998], 573). One can receive only that which has never been given: "I know nothing more despicable than a man whose heart and attentions can be bought, unless it is the woman who pays for them; but between two united hearts community of property is justice and duty, and if I find myself still in arrears with respect to the portion I hold above ours, I accept without scruple what I retain, and owe you what I have not given you" (Rousseau, *Julie, or The New Heloise*, vol. 6 of *The Collected Writings of Rousseau*, ed. Jean Vaché, trans. and annotated Philip Stewart and Jean Vaché [Hanover, NH: University Press of New England, 1997], 55). However, following the model I have just described, Marion is not only forced by Rousseau to give him what he himself wanted to give to her, but in a sense she also becomes indebted for a wrongdoing committed by Rousseau. This is why it is as difficult for Rousseau to accept Marion's gift as it is for him to expiate his wrongdoing. The receipt of this gift was, so to speak, accompanied by a crowd of anonymous avengers who, throughout his life, have not ceased to make him repay his debt dearly. "If, as I venture to believe, such a crime can be expiated, it must surely have been so by the many misfortunes that burden my old age; by forty years of rectitude and honour in difficult circumstances; indeed, poor Marion has found so many avengers in this world that, however grave my offence against her, I am not too afraid that I will carry the guilt for it into the next" (Rousseau, *Confessions*, 85).

43. Cf. de Man, *Allegories of Reading*, 284.

44. A biased judgment is always at the origin of a secret desire, which seeks to find the accused guilty, as can be seen in Rousseau, *Dialogues*, 57: "What happens if instead of assuming here a judge of perfect integrity and without passion, I assumed he was animated by a secret desire to find the accused guilty, and to be seeking only plausible means to justify his partiality in his own eyes?" See also ibid., 29 and 64. Not saying everything is saying nothing, and in this case it is an act of lying: "At most, the most sincere are truthful in what they say, but they lie by their reticence, and what they keep silent about changes what they pretend to admit so much, that by saying only a part of the truth they do not say anything" (Rousseau, *The Neuchâtel Preface to the "Confessions" of J.-J. Rousseau*, vol. 5 of *The Collected Writings of Rousseau*, ed. Christopher Kelly, Roger D. Masters, and Peter G. Stillman; trans. Christopher Kelly [Hanover, NH: University Press of New England, 1998], 586).

45. Rousseau, *Confessions*, 83, emphasis added.

46. I am thus making a distinction between this desire to give and what Paul de Man calls Marion's desire, as a desire for substitution between Rousseau and Marion (De Man, *Allegories of Reading*, 292–293). This desire to give would not reduce its occurrence to a simple reciprocal change of places (between the one who gives and the one who steals) but would instead concern first and foremost the systematic inversion of authorities (between this change of places defined as fiction and the act of reading as a critical aspect of an accusation).

47. Rousseau, *Confessions*, 170, emphasis added. [Translation modified.—Trans.]

48. De Man, *Allegories of Reading*, 293. In reality, the reader's mechanism of lying involves the power to link an isolated moment to other moments, to connect different moments, to the point of creating relations of cause and effect between different points in time, and thus to the point of producing a tangible and effective extension between that which is said at that

moment, that which had to be promised earlier, and that which will henceforth need to be upheld. In this case, too, the child is proposed as a model: "The child hardly can lie when he commits himself; for, thinking only how to get out of a situation at that very present, every means which does not have a present effect becomes of no difference to him. In promising for a future moment, he promises nothing, and his imagination, still dormant, does not know how to extend his being over two different moments in time" (Rousseau, *Emile*, 236). [Translation modified.—Trans.] And this is precisely why innocence will remain pure, unadulterated by the reader's machinations: "All the ups and downs of fate and all men's machinations have little hold over a man like me. In order for any suffering to last, the cause would have to be constantly renewed. For any pause, no matter how brief, is enough for me to regain composure" (Rousseau, *Reveries*, Eighth Walk, 93). Similarly, Rousseau writes: "If only this moment would last for ever" (ibid., Sixth Walk, 55). For other instances of this moment and on the refusal of succession, see Rousseau, *Confessions*, 628–629; Rousseau, *Dialogues*, 157; Rousseau, *Discourse on the Origin*, 26–27. Cf. Jean Starobinski, *The Living Eye*, trans. Arthur Goldhammer (Cambridge, MA: Harvard University Press, 1989), 54–57.

49. "But read all these passages with the sense they present naturally to the mind of the reader and that they had in the mind of the author when he wrote them. Read them in context, with what precedes and what follows; consult the disposition of heart into which these readings put you. It is this disposition that will clarify their true sense for you" (Rousseau, *Dialogues*, 28–29 and 82). On the reader's decision, see also Rousseau, *The Banterer*, vol. 12 of *The Collected Writings of Rousseau*, trans. and ed. Christopher Kelly (Hanover, NH: University Press of New England, 2007), 28. "If only faults like those are imputed to me, I will not defend myself against them any more than simple errors. I cannot affirm not having committed such, because I am not an Angel. But those faults that one claims to find in my Writings may very well not be there, because those who find them there are not Angels either" (Rousseau, *Letters Written from the Mountain*, vol. 9 of *The Collected Writings of Rousseau*, ed. Christopher Kelly and Eve Grace, trans. Christopher Kelly and Judith R. Bush [Hanover, NH: University Press of New England, 2001], 138).

50. [In Rousseau's text, "to compare is to judge."—Trans.] "Profession of Faith of the Savoyard Vicar," in Rousseau, *Emile*, 430 and 442. This idea is also expressed in Rousseau, *Emile*, 355: "Since the more men know, the more they are deceived, the only means of avoiding error is ignorance. Do not judge, and you will never be mistaken." Cf. de Man, *Allegories of Reading*, 232.

51. Rousseau, *My Portrait*, 39. Cf. Rousseau, *Confessions*, 153.

52. Here we can compare Rousseau's reader-liar to the drive for truth as a desire to lie in Nietzsche's "On Truth and Lying" (1873), in *Friedrich Nietzsche on Rhetoric and Language*, ed. and trans. with a critical introduction by Sander L. Gilman, Carole Blair, and David J. Parent (New York: Oxford University Press, 1989), esp. 250.

53. Rousseau, *Confessions*, 58, emphasis added. "I should like to make my mind, as it were, transparent to the reader, and I am therefore trying to display it from every angle, to show it in every light, and to ensure that there is no movement taking place within it that he does not observe, so that he may be able to judge for himself what principle it is that produces such effects" (ibid., 170); "for if I keep silent about something one will not know me about anything, so much does everything depend on everything else, so much is everything one in my character, and so much does this bizarre and peculiar assemblage need all the circumstances of my life to be well unveiled" (Rousseau, *The Neuchâtel Preface*, 589). See also Rousseau, *My Portrait*, 38. Cf. Starobinski, *Jean-Jacques Rousseau: La transparence et l'obstacle*, esp. 225–239.

54. Rousseau, *Dialogues: On the Subject and Form of This Writing*, 6, emphasis added. Cf. Rousseau, *Dialogues*, 80; Rousseau, *History of the Preceding Writing*, vol. 1 of *The Collected Writings of Rousseau*, ed. Roger D. Masters and Christopher Kelly; trans. Judith R. Bush, Roger D. Masters, and Christopher Kelly (Hanover, NH: University Press of New England, 1990), 252–253; Rousseau, *Reveries*, Ninth Walk, 98; and Rousseau, *The Neuchâtel Preface*, 585. On the specular structure of this sentence and the notion of "sight" as a figure of reading, see Kamuf, "Seeing through Rousseau," in *Signature Pieces*, 100–116. Let us also note that the eye of the reader is a blind eye and thus a misleading one, for it can never on its own see the one it is gazing at by putting itself in the other's place: "As for me, let them see me if they can, so much the better, but that is impossible for them; they will only ever see in my place the J.-J. that they have created for themselves and fashioned to their heart's content, which they can hate at their leisure" (Rousseau, *Reveries*, Sixth Walk, 67).

55. Through the words of the Savoyard vicar, Rousseau thus confesses to the omnipotence of God: "My young friend, I have just recited to you with my own mouth my profession of faith such as God reads it in my heart" (Rousseau, "Profession of Faith of the Savoyard Vicar," in *Emile*, 477). Cf. Henri Gouhier, *Les méditations métaphysiques de Jean-Jacques Rousseau* (Paris: Vrin, 1985), 96–97. Any action arising from the heart would not need a witness for it to be seen and recognized; God will provide one himself (Rousseau, *Emile*, 456) because "he knows that I am innocent" (Rousseau, *Reveries*, Second Walk, 19). There is a direct link between this act of taking God as a witness out of innocence of one's heart and the innocent life of a primitive and virtuous man. "One cannot reflect on morals without taking pleasure in remembering the image of the simplicity of the earliest times. . . . When innocent and virtuous men enjoyed having Gods as witnesses of their actions, they lived together in the same huts" (Rousseau, *Discourse on the Sciences and Arts*, vol. 2 of *The Collected Writings of Rousseau*, ed. Roger D. Masters and Christopher Kelly; trans. Judith R. Bush, Roger D. Masters, and Christopher Kelly [Hanover, NH: University Press of New England, 1992], 16). [Translation modified.—Trans.] Cf. Starobinski, *Jean-Jacques Rousseau: La transparence et l'obstacle*, 22–25.

56. Rousseau, *Confessions*, 642. [Translation modified.—Trans.] All truth coming from the reader would be the product of a plot (cf. Rousseau, *Dialogues*, 85, and Rousseau, *On the Art of Enjoying and Other Fragments*, vol. 12 of *The Collected Writings of Rousseau*, trans. and ed. Christopher Kelly [Hanover, NH: University Press of New England, 2007], 59) orchestrated by a group of spies who surround him (cf. *Dialogues*, 108 and 193–194). See also Bennington, *Dudding: Des noms de Rousseau*, 87.

57. Rousseau, *Confessions*, 5.

FICTIONS OF THE CULTURAL

Jean-Jacques Rousseau and the Body Politic of Democracy

The members of the political state are religious because of the dualism between
individual life and species-life, between the life of civil society and political life.
They are religious in the sense that man treats political life, which is remote
from his own individual existence, as if it were his true life; and in the sense
that religion is here the spirit of civil society, and expresses the separation and
withdrawal of man from man.

Karl Marx, *On the Jewish Question*

Introduction

One of the major projects of modernity has been to develop a radical critique of
its own institutions. It is a grand theologicopolitical project of rationalization,
differentiation, and individualization. It is the desire not only to undertake a
systematic analysis of the internal function of all institutions but also to critique the anthropological conditions on which all authority and legitimation
of meaning are founded. This grand project, that of the world's disenchant-
ment, is far from finished. It continues to spread, in space and in time, or in history. Undeterred, this project continues to renew its logic of social division and
symbolic deinstitutionalization, thereby always internally structuring both the
institutional system of our contemporary society and the critical foundation of
the discourse of the humanities. Yet this project of modernity, which continues
to this day, is in reality the rational reconfiguration of another project. More
specifically, it is a question of realizing socially and accomplishing historically
the old Judeo-Christian project of the division of powers, between human institutions (or idolatrous fabrications) and divine institutions (or the true worship

in spirit). The first great social division separates the political from the theological, the earthly from the heavenly, the immanent from the transcendent. The critical rationality of the moderns shifts, reconfigures, and reproduces this division solely on the social level of history, as a new kind of division, which this time is proper to humans themselves, between the individual and the collective, the private and the public, but also between the same and the other, the identical and the diverse, or between the individual body and the proper name. And for Rousseau, it is precisely at this point, where the human is divided and separated from human, that the issue of the *body politic* of society is in question. One must not only analyze the establishment and the institution, the production and the reproduction of this body, but first and foremost one must question the historical, the psychological, and the social conditions of its own imposture.

I. Nature, Culture, and the Economy of History

The Invention of History: From Nature to Culture

§ 1 The affirmation that all social institutions are human institutions implies not only the desire to delegitimize their authority but, more important, it is an assumption that their meaning can be reconstructed on an entirely different foundation—no longer on the force of a dominant ideology defending an abuse of power but rather on the establishment of a social contract through natural or moral reason. For Rousseau, however, this new objective of history in itself represents the entire paradox of modern times in the land of Christianity. On the one hand, the religion of the Gospel was established through the increasingly radical separation between church and state, between the theological and the political.[1] On the other hand, this same Gospel revealed the true religion of the heart, the natural religion, and morality, which causes each citizen "to love his duties" and makes "virtue reign" among them.[2] According to the Judeo-Christian ideals of modernity, it was thus necessary to separate theological power from political power, to liberate true religion from instituted religions, in order to ultimately found the authority of all institutions solely on the moral power of reason. The religion of the Gospel is not a human, political, or social institution, established by a collective body for the benefit of a local, regional, or national power. The *pure Gospel*, or the religion of Jesus, is both personal and universal. It does not depend on any government, any instituted worship, or any official ceremony. Instead, it is instilled by God himself in the heart of every human, and in this sense he speaks directly to all of humanity.

According to Rousseau, the religion of Jesus, of love and faith, is universal because it expresses the true nature of man, his heart and his internal reason. Jesus's speech and acts not only are addressed to man's heart but speak especially from within that heart: Jesus speaks *to* the heart *from within* the heart. He makes the heart speak, giving it a voice in a sense, in order to transform it into a true temple of the divinity, beyond all institutions:

> What is more, whatever decision you may make, bear in mind that the true duties of Religion are independent of the institutions of men; that a just heart is the true temple of the divinity; that in every country and in every sect the sum of the law is to love God above everything and one's neighbor as oneself; that no religion is exempt from the duties of morality; that nothing is truly essential other than these duties; that inner worship is the first of these duties; and that without faith no true virtue exists.[3]

Inner worship is a human duty to the divinity, and the heart is its temple but also, as we will see, the place of a new sacrifice.

In truth, an entire economy of history is at stake in this temple of the heart. The Gospel revealed not only that all institutions are human and thus founded on the ideology of power, domination, and conspiracy, but it thereby, and more importantly, revealed the true authority of power and the true origin of society. In this sense the religion of Jesus did not establish any new institutions and thus did not form a new power; rather, it revealed the *natural place* where every institution's authority and legitimacy are founded. When Jesus speaks to humans from within their own heart, he unveils to them their true nature. He reveals to them the place where humans can *see* themselves in their own nature. This is why, for Rousseau, the figure of Jesus represents a double model, of life and of thought. On the one hand, Jesus lived solely according to the laws of the heart, and on the other he established the principles of a natural religion. Indeed, for Rousseau, the heart constitutes not only the place of withdrawal into oneself, of relation to or return to oneself, of a presence to oneself, in sorrow, thought, or reverie, but it is also and above all the place, the stage, or the theater where nature's spectacle plays out: "It is in man's heart that the life of nature's spectacle exists. To see it, one must feel it."[4] In short, the heart represents the place or the temple where nature's spectacle is experienced, and at the same time it is itself the life of its spectacle. It is itself the living place where nature sees itself (play out). As the editors of Rousseau's works point out, the original text "says *vue* [sight] in error" instead of *vie* [life]: "It is in man's heart that the *sight* of nature's spectacle exist."[5]

By asserting that man's heart represents not only nature's spectacle but also its place of existence, Rousseau gives it a triple function. As in the triple identity in the *Dialogues*, the heart constitutes at the same time the *stage* where the spectacle plays out, the *actor* who takes part in the spectacle and the *spectator* who watches the actor perform the scene. Hence the desire to transform the heart into a new temple of the divinity, a temple-theater for an actor-spectator of oneself who performs the tragedy of history. This is the great objective of the *Discourse on Inequality*: to describe the development of humanity as a historical tragedy, an accident, a catastrophe, which reveals the entire economy of history, between the natural man and the man of man. In the *Confessions* Rousseau reminds us of its source:

> For the rest of the day, I sought and I found, deep in the forest, the image of those earliest times whose history I was proudly tracing; I did not spare the little lies of men, but dare to lay man's nature bare, to follow the progress of time and of the things that have disfigured this nature, and, comparing man of man with natural man, to show him that in his so-called improvement lay the true source of his wretchedness.[6]

This text alone devises an entire program for a life of writing. Everything is there. Rousseau retreats into the forest not only to discover the earliest times of humans but above all to write this history. It is not in his study, behind a table, with open books but in the middle of the forest that Rousseau traces the history of the first humanity. It is a history in three stages. First, it exposes the *nature* of man and thus defines the essence of the natural man. Then it describes the gradual progress of the things that *disfigured* this nature. Finally, it compares the man of man to the natural man, in order to show that the only cause of evil and suffering of all of humanity resides in this social progress or *improvement* [*perfectionnement*]. In short, the true nature of man was disfigured by the improvement of culture. This well-known hypothesis is a problematic affirmation whose terms must all be thoroughly analyzed. Nonetheless, this hypothesis is very clear. Nature is disfigured. In this sense, retracing the history of the earliest times consists not only in describing the successive *stages* of this deformation but also in reconstructing the multiple and diverse *ways* in which nature disfigures itself as culture. Ultimately, for Rousseau, *comparing* the man of man to the natural man does not mean showing that man's nature has disappeared or wanting to return to the origins of this nature. The aim of this systematic, even methodological comparison is to understand how the natural man became man and thus the ways in which and the conditions on which the natural man *became* a social man. In reality, this question consists in knowing how the nature of man was able to disfigure itself, to transform itself, and even to become rejected while remaining intact within the heart, pure and unaltered, unchanged as it was in the first days of humanity.

§ 2 Tracing history from its earliest times consists, just as in this case, in reconstructing an entire economy of disfigurement. Between a radical destruction and a return to the sources, Rousseau seeks to understand how that which divided human *from* human was ultimately able to return human *to* human. It is the sole movement, the sole history, the sole *condition*, or becoming, that forces humans to leave their first primitive state and allows them to establish the foundation for all social institutions. This justifies the comparison between the natural man and the man of man. However, Rousseau is not trying to compare the primitive human of societies without writing with the civilized human of modern societies. He proceeds in an entirely different way. He certainly wants to "observe the differences in order to discover the properties," but with regard to the present human.[7] He wants to discover how the economy of disfigurement between the natural and the artificial is articulated in the present nature of man.

"For it is no light undertaking to separate what is original from what is artificial in the present Nature of man, and to know correctly a state which no longer exists, which perhaps never existed, which probably never will exist, and about which it is nevertheless necessary to have precise Notions in order to judge our present state correctly."[8] This state of nature no longer exists and perhaps will never exist. How, then, is one to describe its reality, its status or function? Is it a simple normative concept, a criterion of comparison in order to discover the present properties of a state of culture?[9] Rousseau is very clear. Disentangling and distinguishing the original from the artificial is necessary in order "to judge our present state correctly." And this distinction must be made *in* the present nature of man, as a comparison between the natural man and the man of man. In no case must the state of nature be considered as a real and historical situation, in which humans would have lived with humans solely in accordance with the laws of nature. Nonetheless, this state exists, in the nature of man. It is in the present and thus the artificial, social, political, and collective state of humans. In fact, it is only there that it exists, in the artifice of the man of man. In addition, it exists only in the *artificial* and *cultural* sense of humans. In that case, however, it really and truly does exist. Hence the necessity to formulate its concept in order to understand our present state. Rousseau's comparative method thus makes it possible to retrace the earliest times of humanity in the present nature of man and thus to reconstruct the temporal economy of their own disfigurement.

Once again, everything relates back to the question of the heart. When he states that the spectacle of nature is experienced in the heart of man, Rousseau is describing this spectacle as a historical tragedy of disfigurement, of transformation, of "stifling." In this case, however, the heart is both the witness and the victim of this stifling. In a certain sense, for Rousseau, man's heart *experienced* all acts of the tragedy, witnessing and remembering the entire historical scene of the fall, of the accident, between a state of nature, in which humans are left to themselves, reduced to the forces of their own body, and the construction of the body politic, in which a human is both separated from and dependent on a human. Yet, in order to reconstruct the concept of the natural man, one can simply look within the heart of men. Most important, one must listen to "the voice of nature" within the heart. This is the *natural law*.

> Leaving aside therefore all scientific books which teach us only to see men as they have made themselves, and meditating on the first and simplest operations of the human Soul, I believe I perceive in it two principles anterior to reason, of which one interests us ardently in our well-being and our self-preservation, and the other inspires in us a natural repugnance to see any sensitive Being perish or suffer, principally those like ourselves. It is from the conjunction and combination that our mind is able to make of these two Principles, without the necessity of introducing that of sociability that all the rules of natural right appear to me to flow: rules which reason is later forced to reestablish upon other foundations when, by its successive developments, it has succeeded in stifling Nature.[10]

Rousseau postulates that God himself has inscribed two natural principles in the heart of man: self-preservation and the respect for the other. However, this is where this question becomes problematic. First, how will the mind connect these two principles? Without presupposing the slightest social or collective determination, the way in which the natural man combines his own self-preservation and the respect for the other will directly produce the "rules of natural right." These rules thus represent the first expression, or they express the first articulation between these two natural principles. This is the first stage in a relation that for now is still natural, between oneself and the other, between identity and difference. This is the first regulation of difference in identity and of identity in difference. Next comes the upheaval of history, the long dialectical process of nature and reason. On the one hand, reason, "by its successive developments," "has succeeded in stifling Nature." To stifle it is to subvert its laws, to appropriate its powers, and even to deny or reject its existence. On the other hand, however, "reason is later forced to reestablish [these rules] upon other foundations." According to the dialectical interpretation by Hegel and Marx, reason preserves that which it denies. The objectives are the same, but the means are completely different. Rousseau understands this *Aufhebung*, or sublation, as a gesture of divine providence. "By considering what we would have become abandoned to ourselves, we ought to learn to bless him whose beneficent hand, correcting our institutions and giving them an unshakeable base, has prevented the disorders which must otherwise have resulted from them, and has created our happiness from the means that seemed likely to reduce our misery."[11]

The double operation of reason, this dialectic of history, which stifles nature and at the same time reestablishes its law on new foundations, is a rectification *foreseen* by the goodness of God. From then on, the rational establishment of social and political institutions will signify both the cause of our misery and the salvation of our own existence. Just as suffering must be treated with suffering, social institutions must be rectified by the institutions themselves. This is, at least, what was foreseen by God. It was thus foreseen, foretold, and preconceived that, in the course of history, the rejection of the laws of nature be reestablished in the constitution of a legitimate body politic. This foresight rectifies what we could have become, on the impetus of reason that is still abusive. In other words, reason is both *abuse* and *salvation*. It is the abuse *of* institutions and the salvation *by* institutions. More important, it is the "successive development" between the disfigurement of nature and the establishment of a body politic. This operation is one and the same, an economy that is one and the same, one single spectacle, in which nature disfigures and reconfigures itself *proportionately to* the constitution of the body politic. In this sense, one could claim that the body politic alone represents the social reconstruction of a disfigurement of nature. This body not only reestablishes the laws of nature on a rational foundation but also represents the reconstructed body of a degraded, abused, and ruined nature, a collective reconstitution of the natural man, torn between himself and the other, between the same or the identical and the different. The legitimate body politic is the social unit of the survival of humans left to themselves, to the dangers of their own alterity.

The Institutions of Law

§ 1 "I assume that men have reached the point where obstacles to their self-preservation in the state of nature prevail by their resistance over the forces each individual can use to maintain himself in that state. Then that primitive state can no longer subsist and the human race would perish if it did not change its manner of living."[12] As in the *Discourse*, it is not "historical truths" but "hypothetical and conditional reasonings" that the *Social Contract* seeks to produce.[13] In this text Rousseau's hypothesis is twofold. On the one hand, in order to overcome the obstacles that threaten its existence, humanity must transform its way of being. This is an important hypothesis in both the *Discourse* and the *Social Contract*. On the other hand, however, these obstacles are both the cause of the transformation of the human and the first harmful effects of the development of humanity. "I assume that men have reached the point." This *point* represents the historical and determined position of an evolution, where the natural powers of the human cannot *resist* everything that threatens his or her self-preservation. Yet this point of conflict between resistance to obstacles and the powers of one's own body—I will return to the term "resistance"—constitutes, most importantly, a shift between two economies of history. That which drove humans to this point of restriction originates from a contingent development, from occasional circumstances, and by accident. However, everything that resulted from this restriction is a matter of necessity, survival, and salvation.

In other words, according to Rousseau, humans could very well have not reached this point of restriction. Staying the way they are, humans could have not developed certain faculties that they have by nature. The hand of God instilled a faculty within the human mind that distinguishes human from animal. This, according to Rousseau, is *perfectibility*, a "distinctive and almost unlimited faculty."[14] It is an ability of generalization and abstraction, of nominalization, which sacrifices the concrete for the abstract, the part for the whole, the singular for the general, the sensible for the intelligible.[15] In fact, it is a power that has three attributes. First, it is a faculty that nothing of immanence, with the exception of external and fortuitous circumstances, made it necessary to be developed. Then, once it is developed by numerous fatal and unforeseen accidents, this faculty becomes the faculty of all faculties, which "successively develops all the others."[16] Finally, it represents the source of all human misfortune.[17]

> After having shown that *perfectibility*, social virtues, and the other faculties that Natural man had received in potentiality could never develop by themselves, that in order to develop they needed the chance combination of several foreign causes which might never have arisen and without which he would have remained eternally in his primitive constitution, it remains for me to consider and bring together the different accidents that were able to perfect human reason while deteriorating the species, make a being evil while making him sociable, and from such a distant origin finally bring man and the world to the point where we see them.[18]

This *point* at which we see humans today, this situation of the present human, corresponds precisely to the historical development of a state of restriction, or the revelation of an obstacle, which had to force humans to change their nature. Here I would like to insist on this "point." Nothing in the nature of humans could force them to change their way of being. Even the faculty of improvement, abstraction, generalization, nominalization, that humans received naturally and as something that is proper to them, in order to distinguish them from animals, could not *on its own* alter this nature. Once developed, however, by a "fatal accident," and thus once its power is put into action, the successive improvement of reason necessarily produces a disaster for humans and society.[19] However, the insistence on this point of rupture between an unfortunate contingency and a necessity of history amounts, first and foremost, to linking these two possibilities of existence. Without the "foreign causes" that developed this faculty, man "would have remained eternally in his primitive constitution." In other words, following Rousseau's hypothetical reasoning, this primitive condition does not only designate the reconstruction of an abstract norm of comparison between the natural man and the man of man. It is first and foremost a *possible world* that does not exist or no longer exists but that could have lasted eternally.[20] Yet this possible world, or this possible infinite continuity of a primitive condition, allows Rousseau to construct the crux of his argumentation, which not only links the *Discourse* to the *Social Contract* but also creates an entire field of reciprocity between literature and politics or, more precisely, between the autobiographical narrative and political economy.

The simple fact that the primitive condition of the human could have persisted allows Rousseau to postulate *moral existence* within the heart of the human and to affirm its *social reestablishment* by the constitution of a legitimate body politic. In both cases it is a matter of survival. Even though humans separated themselves progressively from the state of nature, this state is a "nature . . . [that] nothing destroys," as Rousseau writes in his *Letter to Beaumont*.[21] For in the ideality of a possible world, nature continues to exert its living forces within the heart of the human. There, as we saw earlier, it continues to live out its own spectacle. Despite being stifled by the improvement of reason, rejected by the power of social institutions, nature remains intact within the heart, pure, unaltered, and untouched, as in the earliest times. However, this purity of a nature that protects itself within the heart of man does not protect man from man. It only provides the conditions for the social survival of humans with humans. That which survives within man, the nature that survives in the artificial man, to the extent that we are witnessing today, determines for Rousseau the conditions of possibility (this is the word) of a legitimate body politic, a true collective body, in which man can live with man in justice and legality. This is the main point: how does one link a state of nature, which survives in complete purity within the heart of man, to the establishment of a body politic, which is instituted as a form of survival of a humanity that is destined to disappear.

It cannot be reiterated enough. Rousseau is not pleading for a *return to* the state of nature. On the contrary, what he wants to analyze directly concerns the conditions of a *return of* nature itself. As in Freud, what is considered as "truth" is the conditions that allow the repressed, the rejected, the mutilated, the stifled to return in order to structure the entire psychological and social field of repression. Indeed, for Rousseau, any history of political institutions, and then of natural right, renews the violence of the first moment of stifling or repression. In this sense, a political constitution always corresponds to the social institution of violence and thus of injustice, inequality, and imposture.[22] However, this state of nature, which could have continued to exist in the world but which persists only deep down in the heart, structures all on its own an entire institutional economy of providence, between the fall and salvation, loss and gain, accident and reparation, dissolution and correction, suffering and compensation. In the second part of the *Discourse* (as he had in fact already announced), Rousseau develops different accidents and external causes that made it possible for the improvement of reason to institute a right to inequality that by nature makes the *strong rich* and the *weak poor*. This is the shift from the first imposture, the first agent of this fatal accident, who would have said before the common land "this is mine," to the first legislator, who would have established before the assembly a true right to property, for the beginning of "perpetual war."[23] "Nascent Society gave way to the most horrible state of war," writes Rousseau.[24] From the impostor to the legislator, there is only a step within the succession of fortuitous causes. However, this is a step of progressive war, which announces already, or reveals and shows, what divine providence has *foreseen* in order to modify the course of the objective, the accident, the catastrophe. This is the messianic and prophetic declaration of the *crisis* of human institutions. This is the crisis or the revolution of everything that humans have instituted in order to divide man from man: "We are approaching a state of crisis and the age of revolutions. Who can answer for what will become of you then? All that men have made, men can destroy. The only ineffaceable characters are those printed by Nature; and Nature does not make princes, rich men, or great Lords."[25]

§ 2 The process of writing that leads from the *Discourse* to the *Social Contract* is developed from a foundation of crisis. The attribution of the causes of inequality to the foundation of any social institution is already an act of submitting these institutions to their own future crisis. What Rousseau wants to show in both of these texts is the existence of a relation or a certain economy of history between the first rupture, from a primitive condition to social institutions, and a state of crisis that is internal and proper to all institutions. This is an economic relation because whatever is produced by or destroyed within the institutions directly concerns their own constitution. Every social institution is established by the constitution of a body politic. At the same time, however, this very constitution already contains the causes of its own destruction.[26] As we have seen, this body represents the historical substitution and the collective salvation of the natural man. In other words, it is a social body of survival, a body of sacrifice, which is constructed in three stages: from the first mutilation to the social pact, and from the social pact to its ultimate dissolution. The first principles are already set in the *Discourse*:

> Those most capable of anticipating the abuses were precisely those who counted on profiting from them; and even the wise saw the necessity of resolving to sacrifice one part of their freedom for the preservation of the other, just as a wounded man has his arm cut off to save the rest of his Body.

Such was, or must have been, the origin of Society and Laws, which gave new fetters to the weak and new forces to the rich, destroyed natural freedom for all time, established forever the Law of property and inequality, changed a clever usurpation into an irrevocable right, and for the profit of a few ambitious men henceforth subjected the whole human Race to work, servitude, and misery.[27]

It is a question of the subjugation of humanity by the establishment of the law. It is a question of the alienation of all for the establishment of social freedom. However, what interests me here above all is the question of *sacrifice*, which calls for a double rhetorical figure: a synecdoche, between the part and the whole, and an analogy, between the individual body and the body politic. The origin of society and its laws is a question of sacrifice. When the wisest saw that humans had reached such a level of restriction that they needed to change their nature in order to survive, they decided to "sacrifice one part of their freedom for the preservation of the other." In order to avoid perishing and disappearing completely, with regard to the species, and thus to transform their way of being or their nature, humans sacrificed their natural freedom. As it is stated in the *Social Contract*: "What man loses by the social contract is his natural freedom and an unlimited right to everything that tempts him and that he can get; what he gains is civil freedom and the proprietorship of everything he possesses."[28] However, following the sacrificial language of the *Discourse*, losing one's natural freedom in order to gain civil freedom or one's individual will for the general will is, according to the *Social Contract*, an act of mutilating one's own body, "as a wounded man has his arm cut off to save the rest of his Body."[29] And it is here, already in the *Discourse*, that the synecdoche coincides with the analogy. The social pact or contract is the unity of the body politic, and in this sense it already constitutes the establishment of a collective sacrifice: "Without entering at present into the researches yet to be undertaken concerning the Nature of the fundamental Compact of all Government, I limit myself, in following common opinion, to consider here the establishment of the Body Politic as a true Contract between the People and the Chiefs it chooses for itself; a Contract by which the two Parties obligate themselves to observe Laws that are stipulated in it and that form the bonds of their union."[30]

The analogy between the individual body and the collective body is based on the bonds that link the parts to the whole. The body politic is an organic, living body, "similar to that of man."[31] In his *Discourse on Political Economy*, and following an old analogy, Rousseau attributes a head to this body, a soul to the sovereign body, and organs to the law, represented by the judges and the magistrates. The citizens are its members; industry and agriculture are the mouth and the stomach "that prepare the common subsistence."[32] Finally, the economy is the blood that is distributed "throughout the body," thus giving it movement and life.[33] This is where the question of sacrifice, mutilation, and dismemberment arises. The constitution of the body politic by the social contract is a sacrificial substitution for the survival of the individual body. Henceforth, in order to survive, the individual body, one's own body, the entire body, having reached this point of restriction, must itself become a member of a larger body. It must transform itself into a part of a superior whole. Above all, however, it must sacrifice itself in the sole objective of preserving itself or of surviving within a collective. The *individual body* is the injured member that must be amputated or mutilated "to save the rest of [the] Body." The first version of the *Social Contract* spoke of "mutilation," which the definitive edition would change to "alienation":

> One who thinks he is capable of forming a People should feel that he can, so to speak, change human nature. He must transform each individual, who by himself is a perfect and solitary whole, into a part of a larger whole from which this individual receives, in a sense, his life and his being. He must in a sense *mutilate* man's constitution in order to strengthen it; substitute a partial and moral existence for the physical and independent existence we have all received from nature. He must, in short, take away all man's own, innate forces in order to give him forces that are *foreign* to him and that he cannot make use of without the help of others. Now the more these natural forces are dead and destroyed, and the acquired ones great and lasting, the more the institution as well is solid and perfect.[34]

According to Rousseau, this person, who wants to form a people, is the legislator, the founder of the law or of the soul of the body politic. Whereas the social pact gave life to the body politic, the legislator gives it the will and the movement in order to preserve its existence.[35] This is why legislation or the establishment of laws represents the movement by which the life of the body politic is preserved. However, this preservation, this duration, the time of the existence of the body politic, is founded or constructed on the mutilation of the individual body. This is the sacrificial function of the legislator and his divine or religious power, "beyond all human force."[36] In the text that I have just quoted, we can distinguish between two successive parts as the ritual description of a true sacrifice. This is still the same point of rupture, between nature and culture, between the natural man and the man of man. To found a people, a body of people, one must change its nature, and in order to transform this nature, one must sacrifice it through an act of mutilation. This is what the first part of the text describes. The individual body, which the human received from nature as a perfect and autonomous whole, must not only become a part or a member of a larger whole, of the body politic, but also and especially it is from this larger body that it will henceforth receive its life, its being, its existence and subsistence. By becoming a *member* of the body politic, every person *exchanges* their individual life for collective survival. This is the foundation itself of a political economy. The natural constitution of humans is mutilated, and in this sense the individual is no longer the unity of the parts but rather becomes him or herself the *dismembered* part of an instituted body that gives or gives back to the individual their own existence. This is what the end of the text recalls. In truth, it is a question of an economy between natural forces and instituted forces. Mutilated, dismembered, the individual witnesses the substitution of foreign and acquired forces with his or her own, innate forces. The individual body is a mutilated one in the sense that each of his or her forces is no longer linked to the parts that it consists of and of which the individual is a whole, but rather each force itself *represents* the member of a collective body that is foreign to it. However, not only do these new forces alienate the individual, he or she cannot do anything "without the help of others," but also the life of the alienating and mutilating forces depends directly on the death of the individual and natural forces: "the more these natural forces are dead and destroyed, and the acquired ones great and lasting, the more the institution as well is solid and perfect." In other words, that which constitutes, preserves, and at the same time maintains the unity of a body politic *depends* directly on that which kills or annihilates the natural forces of the individual body. This dependence signifies the destiny of the body politic. The unity of its institutions could last, persist, or preserve its own collective existence only if it can continually annihilate the living forces of the individual body by maintaining it in a state of dismemberment.

II. The Body Politic and the Discourse of Fiction

The Fictional Reconstruction of the Social Body and Natural Religion

§ 1 The body politic, or the collective body, is a paradoxical one. I would even say that, on its own, it constitutes, in its form, function, and power of representation, the main paradox of modern times in the land of Christianity. Indeed, all of modernity is founded on the ideal identity of an autonomous body politic, a Leviathan monster-machine, constructed entirely by the rationality of those of whom it is composed. A gigantic *collective autoreferential fiction*, whose actors are narrators just as much as the narrators are actors. For Rousseau—one of the most important agents of modernity but also its most formidable critic and victim—the body politic is a paradoxical fiction. On the one hand, this fiction is necessary for the survival of the natural body. In this sense, the construction or the constitution of the body politic transforms it into a real, existing body, composed of a head, a soul, organs, limbs, and blood. On the other hand, however, this fiction fails in the autonomy of its constitution, in the authority of its foundation, and thus in its usurpation of sovereignty and in its imposture. This fiction never manages to totally efface or dissimulate the origin from which the unity of the body politic was constituted, and on which its so-called legitimate authority was founded. This paradox, which is also the weakness, the crisis, or the revolution of social institutions and collective establishments, depends directly on the systematic and necessary dismemberment of the individual body, on the rejection of both the living forces and their distribution as political power.

"All that men have made, men can destroy." In other words, every social or human institution contains within it the principle of its own destruction or the causes of its dissolution. Every institution that humans have created can be destroyed by the sole principles of this creation. It is precisely of this crisis that Rousseau speaks—a crisis that reveals not only its ideological and symbolic foundation but also the entire fictional mechanism of substitution. By revealing the sacrificial operation, through the mutilation of the individual body, its dismemberment, alienation, and rejection, Rousseau indicates its limitations, weaknesses, failures, with the aim of a general reconsideration of the relations between nature and society. In other words, the paradox of the body politic reveals a certain *dysfunction* in the economy of sacrifice. On the one hand, social institutions are founded on the substitution of the living forces with the collective forces. The more these natural, innate forces are dead, the more the collective, acquired ones are lasting and solid. On the other hand, however, despite all of the powers of substitution, despite the symbolic rigor of mutilation or alienation, despite the power of rejection or stifling, absolutely nothing of nature and its forces could destroy itself. The alienation of nature's living forces only represents a displacement, a transfer of forces, but a transfer that transforms its power, from a quantitative to a qualitative one. The point at which the sacrificial dismemberment was supposed to substitute the living forces with the collective ones, once mutilated, alienated, and stifled, these same living forces transform, reconstruct, or rearrange themselves. In a certain sense, they transform physical and quantitative powers related to the parts of a body that is now dismembered or divided into qualitative, psychological, and moral powers related to the movements of the soul and the heart, which becomes the new place where nature experiences its own spectacle but also the new temple where a new sacrifice can be made.

This could be considered as a crisis or even a failure of the body politic to constitute itself: a fiction that expresses the paradoxes of every social institution. For Rousseau, the state of nature is indestructible. Even though they are generally and continually alienated or rejected, the living forces remain as pure as they were in the earliest times. This again recalls Freud. In Rousseau, however, these forces are always exerted in order to reveal, to make visible and manifest, the *imposture* on which the authority of the law, the general will, and social institutions is founded. Even though the establishment of laws is necessary to legitimize the constitution of the body politic, no law can be established without presupposing the use of illegitimate force. This is the irreducible difference between the *establishment* of the law by the legislator and the *use* of the law by the people, as discussed in the *Social Contract*:

> In order for an emerging people to appreciate the healthy maxims of politics, and follow the fundamental rules of Statecraft, the effect would have to become the cause; the social spirit, which should be the result of the institution, would have to preside over the founding of the institution itself; and men would have to be prior to laws what they ought to become by means of laws. Since the Legislator is therefore unable to use either force or reasoning, he must necessarily have recourse to another order of authority, which can win over without violence and persuade without convincing.[37]

This text thus expresses the whole difference between the establishment of the law by the legislator, its application by the government, and the people's adherence to it. How can the legitimate establishment of the law construct a government proper to its application without itself becoming the institution of this government?[38] This is the concrete and institutional expression of the paradoxes of the body politic, which Rousseau describes as evident contradictions: "The difficulty lies in understanding how there can be an act of Government before the Government exists, and how the People, which is only Sovereign or subject, can become Prince or Magistrate in certain circumstances. Here, again, is revealed one of those amazing properties of the body politic, by which it reconciles apparently contradictory operations. For in this case, the operation is accomplished by a sudden conversion of Sovereignty into Democracy."[39] This sudden conversion consists in instituting a temporary or "provisional Government," which dissolves itself instantaneously or at least represents the ideality of "a Government without a Government."[40] This is a government that never creates a *body*—it is, in a sense, a body without a body. "If there were a people of Gods, it would govern itself Democratically. Such a perfect Government is not suited to men."[41] In addition, conceived as the ideal institution of a democracy, this moment of conversion inevitably becomes the moment of the usurpation of power: "all the governments of the world, once they are invested with the public force, sooner or later usurp the Sovereign authority."[42] Hence the *necessity* for the legislator to have recourse "to another order of authority, which can win over without violence and persuade without convincing."

In the case that a true democratic government cannot be achieved within this time, in the continuity of history, and thus if a body politic whose established power coincides perfectly with the act of the general will cannot be instituted, the great, the true legislator, the founder, in order to make sure that the law is respected will henceforth need to have recourse to the authority of "sublime reason" that is inaccessible to human reason.[43] If reality cannot be constituted and the unity of a democratic body cannot be maintained, the legislator will necessarily need to use superior force. This is what tradition would call the authority of divine institutions, which the legislator and he alone has access to and whose secret only he knows. More important, the genius of the legislator lies in the reign of or the respect for its authority: "the true miracle that should prove his mission."[44] For Rousseau, this miracle does not concern the temporary authority of political laws but more specifically the indestructible force of the laws of the heart or the laws of nature. Beyond all laws, there is only one:

> which is not engraved on marble or bronze, but in the hearts of the citizens; which is the *genuine constitution of the State*; which gains fresh force each day; which, when other laws age or die out, *revives* or *replaces* them, preserves a people in the spirit of its institution, and imperceptibly *substitutes* the force of habit for that of authority. I am speaking of morals, customs, and especially of opinion—a part of the laws unknown to our political thinkers, but on which the success of all the others depends; a part to which the great Legislator attends *in secret* while appearing to limit himself to the particular regulations that are merely the sides of the arch of which morals, slower to arise, form at last the unshakable Keystone.[45]

§ 2 Every word of this superb and terrifying text deserves an in-depth analysis. Rousseau describes the laws of the heart. As opposed to the political laws engraved on marble by human institutions, these laws are inscribed in the heart by nature or by God himself. This is why they constitute the foundation of the authority of political laws, "the genuine constitution of the State." In themselves they do not establish any legal prescription, any positive right, but rather they institute the spirit of the law, or that which "preserves a people in the spirit of its institution." And these laws of nature, according to Rousseau, are genuine forces that are renewed every day. These are forces of preservation, vitalization, and replacement. These are not physical or bodily forces, related to the parts and actions of the body, but rather psychological and moral forces, related to customs, habits, and opinion. This is where all of the legislator's quasi-religious activity takes place. In fact, this activity is double, for an impossible mission "beyond human force." On the one hand, it is a question of political and social work, apparent and visible, which restores positive laws, as a legitimate undertaking of the general will. On the other hand, however, the gap between the institution of the law and its application is irreducible, the constitution of a social body of the democracy is always deficient, and the usurpation by the government is inevitable. This is the reason for this other authority of the legislator, faint, silent, and secret, which shapes the laws of the heart that are already there, already engraved by the forces of nature. For the grand legislator, secretly shaping these forces is a way to steer customs and restrict public opinion in order to make virtue, or the "conformity of the private will to the general," reign.[46]

For Rousseau, there is no difference between the secret activity of the legislator and that of the priest of a natural religion, as it is the case with the Savoyard vicar. The one and the other, the one just as the other, directly affect the laws of the heart. The last chapter of the *Social Contract* is entitled "On Civil Religion." Along with the *Profession of Faith*, this text constitutes the main reason for the plot against Rousseau, the accusation of impiety brought against him, and especially the essential cause for the decree for his arrest [*prise de corps*]. Earlier I quoted the vicar's affirmations concerning the duties of the true religion, which are independent of human institutions, and those relating to the heart as "inner worship," or the "true temple of the divinity." According to the *Social Contract*, this true religion is the religion of Jesus, who "came to establish a Spiritual kingdom on earth. By separating the theological system from the political system, this brought about the end of the unity of the State, and caused the internal divisions that have never ceased to stir up christian peoples."[47] According to Rousseau, this is the reason for the conditional necessity of not making the religion of the heart, or the natural religion, that of Jesus or of pure Gospel, a civil or national religion. As we have seen, this religion is both personal, inscribed in the heart of everyone, and universal, and thus common to all humans. As Rousseau states in the *Letters Written from the Mountain*—in which he responds to the accusations of impiety—"perfect Christianity is the universal social institution."[48] On the one hand, this is a *social* institution that makes virtue and the love of one's neighbor reign. On the other hand, however, this is a *universal* institution that does not depend on the constitution of a state, a nation, or a country [*patrie*]. "The Christian Religion, through the purity of its morality, is always good and healthy in the State, provided that it is not made a part of its constitution, provided that it is allowed there uniquely as Religion, sentiment, opinion, belief. But as political Law, dogmatic Christianity is a bad establishment."[49]

We can see that Rousseau's argumentation is developed on a double plan of analysis. This is the old theologicopolitical problem, which is reconsidered here in relation to the question of the heart. Rousseau seeks to radically separate the theological institutions of the true religion and the political institutions of the state. The first are moral and universal, with the aim of educating people by "inspiring humanity"; the latter are dogmatic and national, intended to educate citizens and inspire patriotism. And this is where the figure of the legislator reappears: "Patriotism and humanity, for example, are two virtues incompatible in their energy, and especially among an entire people. The Legislator who wants them both will get neither one nor the other. This compatibility has never been seen and never will be, because it is contrary to nature, and because one cannot give the same passion two aims."[50] This is the tragedy of the legislator: he can never truly accomplish his mission. He will never be able to make humanity and citizenship, customs and citizenship, morality and politics, the living forces of the heart and the collective forces of society coincide totally and perfectly. Yet this analysis recalls once again the necessary separation between church and state, but here it already indicates the limitations of the political self-constitution or the democratic constitution of the state, thereby revealing, at the height of the Enlightenment, the flaws in the unity of an autonomous and sovereign body politic.

This is why Rousseau ultimately wants to link the natural religion, or the justice of the heart, to social institutions, not in the highly unlikely future of a democratic government but rather as a new consideration of a body politic or a new political condition for a social body. The moment when the inevitable usurpation of the people's sovereignty by the government was to efface, through the supposedly legitimate laws, the gap between their creation and their application—and thus through the diversion of the imposture by its legitimization—, Rousseau insists on this gap in order to reveal the entire economy of rupture between the humanity of the natural man and the citizenship of the political man. The failure of this rupture and especially the possibility for the body politic to dispense with it, and thus to erase its menacing traces and reject the effects of crisis inherent in each of the body politics' institutions, are the reason for Rousseau's analysis. Thus, in the *Social Contract* and in *Emile*, Rousseau seeks to show that the legislation by which the body politic constructs its identity and constitutes itself as a force of domination is an imposture, an individual will that appropriates the general will, an ideological fabrication, a juridical construction, and thus a fictional discourse, but a fiction that is necessary to maintain the unity of the body away or safe from its own founding principles. In this sense, legislation represents a veritable rampart, a great safeguard that protects the unity of the political body from its self-destruction or from the history of its constitution as an imposture. It protects this body by establishing a right that controls the menacing resurgence of the mutilated parts of the individual body. Indeed, for Rousseau, the dogmatic Christian religion, as well as any civil religion, any government, and any national or local legislation, are useful only for controlling the return of the mutilated in order to maintain the legitimate unity, and especially to reproduce the dominant power of the state. He would never be forgiven for demonstrating this.

In my opinion, this is precisely where this matter becomes both astounding and tragic. "They would have been content to relegate the *Social Contract* along with the *Republic* of Plato, *Utopia*, and the *Sevarambes* into the land of the chimeras. But I depicted an existing object, and they wanted to change that object's face. My Book bore witness against the attack they were going to make. That is what they did not pardon me for."[51] This is the attack of the accusers, who want to "burn the book" and to order the arrest [*prise de corps*] of its author. For Rousseau, however, the worst and the most unforgivable of crimes was to have already demonstrated this in his book: as a book, the *Social Contract* had already borne witness to the arrest that the author himself would soon face. In a certain sense, he had already spoken about this and announced the attack in his description of the constitution of the "social contract" as a fundamental pact of the body politic. Furthermore, he traced its history or reconstructed its imposture by describing how the unity and the preservation of such a body were constructed on the mutilation of the individual body, on the destruction of its parts, their alienation, their exploitation, and their rejection, and on the juridical protection from any possible return of the living forces. This explains the desire of the representatives of power to relegate the text to "the land of the chimeras," of fictional beings that are both harmless and nonexistent. However, the act of describing this social mechanism of dismemberment, this veritable sacrifice, in order to reveal the legitimate parameters of the body politic and the inevitable usurpation of power, already provides the conditions necessary for a resurgence of the mutilated forces, or for the return of the repressed. This already involves saying the *truth* about the body politic, telling it *its own* truth, and showing the discursive fiction and the abuse of power on which it is founded, in order to bring to light its imposture. In any case, this is what Rousseau's *Social Contract* shows. What this book shows or demonstrates more specifically is that Rousseau as a person, his being or his life, already reveals this resurgence. This book is his *existence* itself. His individual body "itself" embodies, as a sign or a symptom, a collective and social inscription of a return of the mutilated, an endless crisis or a revolution that has already begun. Hence the necessity to announce his arrest [*prise de corps*], in order to take hold of the resurgence of the mutilated, to control the return of the repressed, and thus to protect the unity of the body politic from the internal causes of its own destruction.

Vitam vero impedenti

§ 1 Facing the warrant for his arrest, Rousseau flees. This is in June 1762, just after the accusation. "I left Paris my heart pained with distress after the Parliament's warrant."[52] In the two drafts of the preface to *The Levite of Ephraim*, Rousseau compares his own situation of exile to the murder of the concubine in the Bible (Judges 19).[53] This takes place in the intermediary period. After conquering the promised land, the people of Israel is still divided into twelve tribes and without a kingdom. At that time, a man, the Levite, takes a woman of low morals as his concubine. One day, however, she becomes angry and leaves him to return to her family. The Levite does not accept this. He undertakes a long voyage, finds her, and manages to convince her father to let her leave. On their way back, the Levite and his concubine spend a night in a city inhabited by the Benjaminites, where they find hospitality. However, just as night falls, a group of bandits attacks the host's house. They want to "know" the Levite. In the tradition of the sacred law of hospitality, the host negotiates with them and offers to them his virgin daughter in exchange. However, the Levite intervenes, takes hold of his concubine, and offers her to the bandits, who abuse her all night. The next morning the Levite finds her dead. The text then says: "When he had entered his house, he took a knife, and grasping his concubine he cut her into twelve pieces, limb by limb, and sent her throughout all the territory of Israel."[54] Here, all of the Hebrew terms evoke a genuine ritual of sacrifice. *Ma'akelet* is the knife that Abraham had to use to sacrifice his son Isaac. The verb *natah*, which means to rip to pieces, to dismember, to cut up, is usually used to describe the preparation of animal sacrifice for Yahve. Finally, the expression *laesemeya*, "bone by bone" or, more literally, "following her bones," in other words, by following the articulation that joins one limb to another, reveals the professional technique of the high priest who conducts sacrifices.

In *The Levite of Ephraim*, Rousseau not only attempts to rewrite this story, this tragedy of tragedies that has no equal in the history of the Hebrew people since the Exodus from Egypt, as the biblical text states, but more importantly he seeks to find in it the solution to his own suffering, consolation or compensation for his own misfortunes.[55] "This is what I occupied myself with during the cruelest moments of my life, overcome with miseries for which an honorable man is not even allowed to prepare himself."[56] To the best of my knowledge, Rousseau never literally compared his own body to the dismembered body of the victim. Yet what he tries to articulate is a certain relation between two necessities: on the one hand, the necessity for the people of Israel to found a political and social unity, "a kingdom," upon the dismembered body of a woman accused of impiety and, on the other hand, the necessity for a body politic of the modern state, "the democracy," to eliminate Rousseau's individual body by accusing him of impiety. These are two necessities but also two failures. The first concerns the destruction of the kingdom and the exile of the people to the desert. The second concerns the defeat of democracy and the alienation of the people by the government. Rousseau's individual body thus becomes the body of a scapegoat for the sake of a body politic that is in a crisis of authority, of sovereignty, and for the sake of the ideals of a modernity that is losing legitimacy. But this is not the worst. The worst is that his cursed, accused, attacked body was used to substitute it with another point of division, mutilation, and dismemberment. This division is proper to modern times and proportionate to the crises of modernity. While on the run and in exile, Rousseau writes *The Levite of Ephraim* with the aim of transforming his arrest [*prise de corps*], and thus the threat of his own dismemberment, into another kind of division of the body, of substituting it for a new condition or situation. "I thought of diverting my reverie by occupying myself with some subject; this one came to mind, and I found it suited enough to my views. It offered me a type of intermediary between the condition I was in and that into which I wished to pass, I could from time to time abandon myself to my somber mood then substitute the sweetest objects for it."[57]

Rousseau speaks of an intermediary situation between two conditions. More specifically, this is a situation of exile, internal and external, but a situation that is described by both the *Letters Written from the Mountain* and *Rousseau, Judge of Jean-Jacques: Dialogues*. In a certain sense, Rousseau now finds himself in the situation of the Levite's concubine after the rape. Like her, he was abused by the plot of impostors, though he did not die from it. He managed to escape, and his individual body was not dismembered. Yet his honor, his freedom, and his life were tarnished.[58] Although his body was not mutilated, his name was tainted nonetheless. This is the historical but also literary shift or transfer from the individual body to the proper name, a transition from bodily dismemberment, "bone by bone," to the psychological split of an identity. This transition is revealed by the biographical event of a publication, which "cuts" Jean-Jacques Rousseau's life into two different individuals, as we can read in the *Dialogues*: "*Rousseau*: You must admit that this man's destiny has some striking peculiarities. *His life is divided into two parts* that seem to belong to two different individuals, with the period that separates them—meaning the time when he published books—marking the death of one and the birth of the other."[59] This is no longer a body that is cut into twelve parts in order to unite the twelve tribes of Israel as a kingdom, but a life that is cut into two parts, split into two people, in order to maintain the representation of unity of the body politic of democracy. These are two individuals: one bears a family name, a birth name, that is Rousseau, while the other has a public name, an author's name, created at the moment that a book becomes public, that is Jean-Jacques.

Henceforth, his life is divided into two parts, two individuals, whereby one cannot see himself without viewing through the eye of the other: "I had necessarily to say how, if I were someone else, I would view a man such as myself."[60] However, for the individual body of Jean-Jacques Rousseau, this division not only represents a veritable split of personality or identity, between the same and the other, but also reveals with regard to the body politic of modernity a real crisis of unity, authority, and legitimacy. Rousseau is a victim, but he in turn also accuses and denounces. Indeed, by this split the whole economy of the first rupture between the natural man and the man of man *returns*, not only to unveil the history of this supposed political self-constitution of the state and thus the history of this imposture, but also and more importantly to shape the threatening future of its own crisis. However, Rousseau is not duped by the impostors' plot. He understood their intention of putting to death the man himself by the slander of his proper name. He detected their scheme to destroy the man, to discredit his honor and his speech, to silence him in order to produce a different man, like a second *public* birth, which both represents and dissimulates the great rupture of history, between the natural man and the man of man. Ultimately, the aim of the plot is to forbid the man who puts his name on the book, who *signs* it, from "responding" for this accusation and thus from making the source visible, from revealing or expressing to all the sacrificial mechanism of the imposture.[61] It seeks to eliminate the dangers that the errant status of a proper name represents to the collective unity, but also to restrict the destructive effects that can arise at the political boundaries between the individual body and the proper name. Above all, however, this plot aims to prevent Rousseau from contaminating the social man or the body politic with the return of the natural man or of the mutilated body. This is precisely where Rousseau enacts the transitional phase, in order to transform his own situation. He "substitute[s] the sweetest objects for" the being divided by the plotted attack, this life split by its "public status" between one individual and another. He substitutes the fictional reconstruction—literary, biographical, or autobiographical—of a *new relation* between himself and nature for the political division of his proper name. Whereas the body politic divided him into an individual body and a proper name in order to protect itself, Rousseau, in order to free himself, transforms this division of existence into a new form of life, a new force of infinite sweetness:

> Once I recovered from that sweet chimera of friendship, the vain search for which caused all the misfortunes of my life, and recovered even more from the errors of opinion of which I am the victim . . . I withdrew into myself, and living between myself and nature, I tasted an infinite sweetness in the thought that I was not alone, that I was not conversing with an insensitive, dead being; that my hardships were finite, my patience was measured, and all the miseries of my life were but title to the compensations and benefits of a better state.[62]

This is the beginning of the *Reveries*, whose aim is to construct a new body, but it is also the achievement of divine providence, which had already been announced in the *Discourse*. Once again, this withdrawal into oneself, between the self and nature, is not a simple return to oneself or a return to nature. It is a question of an economy that is provisional, compensational, and beneficial, which allows for a double movement—of nature. With this withdrawal, not only can nature return or reemerge in its most perfect vitality, but it also returns to form a new state, a new existential relation with the soul or the heart. Indeed, it is in this withdrawal that a force of life "between myself and nature" comes or comes back to reconstitute itself. Here, however, it is not a question of the psychological dimension of an interior life but rather that of a fictional reconstruction of a dead man. This is a dead man who can speak now. This is the writing of a man who has been "buried alive in a coffin."[63] This withdrawal into oneself is thus not a return to nature, to an original state of life, but rather the establishment of a place of death, of a coffin. This is the state of a tomb, which henceforth represents the new constitution of Rousseau's individual body.

§ 2 The great project of the *Reveries* consisted in rigorously establishing a category of operations of the soul. "I shall apply the barometer to my soul," Rousseau writes, in order to know "its state day by day."[64] This is the new state or the new situation so sought after since *The Levite of Ephraim*. This daily state of the soul, day by day, its painful existence, its mockery, its space and time of extreme exhaustion represent a state that is "incapable" [*hors d'état*].[65] This state of the soul has no scruples [*état d'âme*], with the goal of a new relation to life, a *pure living force* "between myself and nature." From the First Walk, Rousseau describes this new situation as an actual killing of the individual body: "a whole generation would by common consent delight in burying me alive."[66] Yet in the face of this act of burying, Rousseau makes a distinction between two attitudes—*resistance* and *resignation*—toward a new division of his own existence. The impostors' plot divided his being into two distinct individuals, an individual body and a proper name, which reproduce and reconstruct but at the same time reveal the first rupture between the natural man and the man of man. At first, in the face of this violence, Rousseau's spontaneous attitude was to resist, to fight for the restoration of unity, honor, and justice. "My distress and indignation plunged me into a frenzy which has taken no less than ten years to subside, during which time, as I reeled from one error to another, from one mistake to another and from one foolish act to another, my reckless behavior gave those who were responsible for my fate all the ammunition that they have so skillfully used to determine it once and for all."[67] For ten years, Rousseau resists, gets angry, ensnares himself; he writes his *Confessions* and his *Dialogues* in order to explain himself, to provide a reply, and in the hopes of passing on his confessions to later generations.[68] He resists for the sake of posterity, for the future, for the memory of his name, and for "the return of the public," this pious collective return of the repressed.[69] He writes in the hopes of a true body politic,

a body of justice, which is established solely on the general will, a future democracy, which will be able to recognize the truth of his discourse and the dignity
of his name. He addresses this messianic body, but in doing so he sinks further
to an unresolvable state of loss. Even though the public or collective body can be
dissolved, transformed by the disappearance and the appearance of new members, its hatred remains immortal. "Individuals may die, but these collective
organizations never die. The same passions thrive in them, and their fervent
hatred, as immortal as the demon who inspires it, remains as active as ever."[70]

The immortal entity or demon of the body politic, its immutable imposture,
not only makes resistance useless and memory illusory but, more importantly,
it transforms them into the grip and instruments of alienation, suffering, and
death. Whereas in the *Social Contract*, as we have seen, Rousseau speaks about
the first point of conflict between the resistance of obstacles and the forces of
the individual body, in the *Reveries* the situation now seems to be reversed.
The resistance of external obstacles has defeated, stifled, or repressed the living
forces, thereby transforming the natural man into a social man for the survival
of the species. Thus, every struggle, every conflict, every resistance to this resistance can only be in favor of the adversaries and benefit the complicity of the
imposture. The tragedy of this war lies in the fact that every resistance fighter
becomes an accomplice. Therefore, for Rousseau, one must no longer resist but
rather resign oneself to remaining in the tomb. And as he relates in the preface
to *The Levite of Ephraim*, this is precisely where this new "state" reemerges, as a
position of a body that remains "buried alive in a coffin," without resistance or
hope for anything else: "An event as sad as it was unforeseen has finally *wiped
out* from my heart this last glimmer of hope and has shown me that my *earthly*
fate is *irrevocably* fixed for evermore. Since then I have resigned myself completely and have found peace again."[71] This event doubtlessly represents the
"unforeseen accident" that Rousseau describes in the Second Walk. Rousseau is
violently knocked down by a dog, his face smashed, his body broken and torn,
blood flowing profusely. All of France was already saying that Rousseau was
dead, "the King himself and the Queen spoke of it as if it were a certainty."[72]
Yet between this murderous accident and this rumor of his death, Rousseau
witnesses his own rebirth, finding a new life or existence. "In that instant I was
born into life."[73] And this rebirth, this "irrevocable" return to life, coincides
with a new form of writing—a new address, a new name, a new signature written directly with this impersonal blood that now flows from Rousseau's broken
[*désœuvré*] body.

This is a new economy of writing that makes it possible to live "between
myself and nature;" an economy that is now founded on the unworking of the
body. "But whereas my body is unworked [*désœuvré*], my soul remains active,

still producing feelings and thoughts, and its inner moral life seems even to have increased with the death of all earthly and temporal interests."[74] Not only is the soul alive in this unworked body, but also and especially the more the body is unworked, stripped, or reduced to its own remains by becoming its own tomb, the more the soul becomes animated. This is the inverse return of the living forces of nature. Whereas the *Discourse* spoke of the necessity, as we can recall, of systematically destroying the living and natural forces of the individual body in order to constitute and preserve the body politic, the *Reveries* describes the necessity of reconstructing these forces through the resignation, the nonresistance, and the unworking of the body. Here lies the difference between the dismembered body and the unworked body. The dismemberment of the body is the foundation of the unity of a body politic, its demonic power and its immortal imposture, toward a collective and symbolic conception of society. On the contrary, the unworking of the body makes a new human possible for another history of humanity, another symbolic relation of collectivity, between the same and the other, the identical and the different. In other words, this is a different conception of the social, no longer built on the collective establishment of meaning. It is a different writing of history that does not write or describe the glorious future of memory, either individual or collective, but rather reveals the conditions for its failure by reconstructing its history in order to *build* the tomb in its place. Rousseau's unworked body, dispossessed of its attributes, left to remain at the bottom of the pit, is itself the tomb of history. It alone unveils and represents the political failure of history, the progressive ruin of its improvement, from the earliest times of humanity, between a state of nature and a state of society. This unworking constitutes a true historical revelation that exhibits and more importantly thwarts any fraudulent strategy and any falsification that humans might have produced in order to efface, in order to dissimilate themselves to themselves, the imposture on which the unity of their body politic is founded.

For Rousseau, however, this unworking of the body corresponds to a fictional state, if not in the sense of a moral fable, a short story, a novel, and thus a literary genre "that pretends."[75] This state is a fiction that does not concern reality and does not address any living being but that speaks already from the place of a dead man. As Rousseau explains, this is a fiction that is elaborated by me for me, which thus creates confusion between fiction and reality: "I absorbed into my fictions all these delightful objects, and, finding myself at last gradually brought back to myself and my surroundings, I could not distinguish between fiction and reality."[76] This fiction, which is produced by the unworking of the body, thus cannot be defined by this separation. It is not part of it. And in this sense, its function does not consist in suspending reality or any *reference* to reality, following a traditional definition of fiction, but rather in reconstructing the reality of a state of death, a state without a state, out of order, which represents not only a new situation of living, of *living forces*, that brings me back to myself, but also a new form of writing. According to Rousseau, this fiction of the "always already dead" and of the "still already living" (even more so once already dead) concerns this coincidence and perhaps even this identical form between its innate nature and a state of nature. Starting from the foreword to the *Discourse*, as we saw earlier, it was difficult "to separate what is original from what is artificial in the present Nature of man, and to know correctly a state which no longer exists, which perhaps never existed, which probably never will exist."[77] At the end of the Eighth Walk, however, this "inexistent" state of nature that survives in the current nature of man, in the vitality of the heart, now constitutes for Rousseau's unworked body the movement of the living forces by which I am brought back to myself:

> All the ups and downs of fate and all men's machinations have little hold over a man like me. In order for any suffering to last, the cause would have to be constantly renewed. For any pause, no matter how brief, is enough for me to regain composure. I am at men's mercy as long as they can have an effect on my senses; but at the first moment of respite, I return to being what nature intended: whatever may happen, that is my most constant state and the one through which, in spite of destiny, I enjoy a kind of happiness for which I feel I was made.[78]

Rousseau does not say that by bringing himself back to himself, and thus by resigning himself to the unworking of his body, nature returns as such or that the natural man reemerges from the political man. Instead, he says that "at the first moment of respite, I return to being what nature intended." Thereby, it is Rousseau "himself" who becomes, or becomes once again, this state of nature, or *what nature intended*. From that moment forward, he himself embodies a new existential relation between himself and nature. His being "itself," his being-tomb, becomes a pure relation of living forces, without a body, without passions, without emotions, with no exteriority; this is a fictional being that is even beyond the traditional opposition between fiction and reality. This is a being that alone expresses, and alone experiences, the *return* of the living forces that nature intended. Therefore, this fiction of the unworked body does not signify a return to a state of nature that has never existed; rather, it represents the historical conditions for the return of a mutilated, dismembered, and repressed body to the unity of the body politic. This is the return of the repressed, which establishes itself in the form of a living force and which thereby comes back to impede "all men's machinations" in order to discredit or delegitimize the authority of political and social institutions. This new salutary state, so sought after by Rousseau, is nothing more than an unworked body, a disembodied living force, which reveals to humanity the whole mechanism and at the same time the whole history of its own imposture.

For Rousseau, the fiction of his own reverie thus must not be defined as a literary genre. This fiction is neither a biography nor an autobiography nor a confession. In fact, it does not even concern the literary question or discursive forms. For this reason, it must not be placed in relation to the classical opposition between literature and reality or within the distinction between literary expression and objective knowledge. This fiction has no literary attributes; no rhetorical, poetic, or narrative function; no address or addressee and thus no public, not even a future one. It does not express any style 'nor develop'? any genre. It does not attempt to perpetuate any memory or seek to commemorate any name, nor does it presuppose any form of reading, the identity of any reader or the identity of any interpreter. And in this sense, Rousseau no longer signs his fictions with his proper name but rather directly with his unworked body. He no longer wants to resist by inscribing his name, in order not to separate "the trial of the Book from that of the man."[79] He no longer wants to attach his name to his body in order to take hold of it, to appropriate it once again, to reincorporate or to reincarnate it, as a way toward a new personal identity and a new enchantment of the world.[80] On the contrary, he wants to allow it to detach itself, to be lost, to err "irrevocably." This means that one must resign oneself to the unworking of the body and produce the irreversible state of detachment from one's name. The unworked body represents an *anonymous* body, one that is expropriated of everything that defines it. It is without a history, without a past or future. It has no property, neither private nor public, neither individual nor collective. Nevertheless, this is indeed a body, but one that is fictional, without a name or authority, a form of pure survival, a counterpart to the body politic of democracy. By separating radically and irrevocably his proper name from his individual body, Rousseau's resignation produces a new form of body as well as a new figure of fiction. It is a *body of fiction* that is created at the boundaries but that also produces and reproduces the boundaries of the individual body and the body politic.

Although this fictional body should have allowed Rousseau to return to himself and thus to return to being "what nature intended" (in other words, a pure living force), this body already creates the possibility for a new history, a new political field, a new world for discourse and representation but also a new "literary space" for texts and writing. Once this anonymous fictional body is established as a tomb, it in turn also becomes *detachable*. It is no longer a question of a proper name that detaches itself from an individual body, as is the case in the traditional Judeo-Christian state of history, in which an individual body is opposed to the body politic, whereby the rupture between the natural man and the political man is instituted as a true social division that separates man from man. Instead, now it is a question of a *new body* that detaches itself from this anonymous, unworked, and expropriated body. From now on, in modernity and until the present day, an entire rationale of social reconstruction and political reproduction of power is at play here with regard to Rousseau's unworked body, between the name, death, and memory. At the heart of a crisis of authority or legitimacy, of sovereignty, on the brink of the revolution, the main question consists in knowing how modern society, or modernity, will be able to reconstitute the conditions necessary for the existence of its own body politic. How will society seize, use, but also invest in everything that threatens to break up the unity of its own body, in order to socially reproduce its political authority? However, in Rousseau's case, or with Rousseau as a starting point, this becomes a question of a new form of social recomposition. It is no longer a name that detaches itself from a body in order to divide the individual in two, but rather it is a new body that is established on an anonymous unworking. It is no longer the memory of a dead man that survives in the social inscription of his name, but instead it is the unworking of the dead man that produces a new condition for the existence of the body. And the entire political strategy of a disenchanted modernity, destined to make up for the ruins of democracy, will consist in seizing this new body, or this new form of life, in order to establish or transform its anonymity into a cultural artifice. It is the establishment of an anonymous body as a *cultural body*. An establishment that allows it once again, and perhaps for the last time, to reproduce the conditions for its existence in order to reorganize a new imposturous plot.

This is the body of *the cultural*, a body of fiction that establishes, just like various cultural inscriptions and practices, the political failures of democracy: a bodily substitute for the body without a body of democracy. But more important, it is the "reality" of the cultural that is constructed on Rousseau's anonymous body, in order to inscribe and establish within it the society of collective unworking. This is a cultural body whose entire Judeo-Christian history remains to be written within and beyond the opposition between nature and culture, between the individual and society. It is not a question of a cultural history, a comparative science of cultures, religions, or mentalities, but a history *of* the cultural, a history that retraces the fabrication of this abstract, detached, unconnected category, this fictional entity, which no longer exists in opposition to nature but which is founded on the failures of an unworked society. In fact, this is a history whose aim is to describe the mechanism of inscription, of transcription, but also of translation between an anonymous body, which is neither dead nor alive, and the defeat of the great critical project of modernity. This is a history of practices, discourses, representations, by which the cultural inscription of an anonymous body was able to *produce* this new social reality of the silent masses or the new plot of the majority, ultimately in order to *reproduce* the political power of an immortal imposture. In other words, this would be a history of silence that protects the ideals of modernity from its own foundations, its failure and its ruin, with the objective of averting its crisis or of establishing what would henceforth be called a *culture of crisis*.

Notes

At the invitation of Geoffrey Bennington, this text was presented at a conference at Emory University, Atlanta, Georgia, in December 2005.

1. Rousseau, *Social Contract*, 217.

2. Rousseau, *Discourse on Political Economy*, vol. 3 of *The Collected Writings of Rousseau*, ed. Roger D. Masters and Christopher Kelly; trans. Judith R. Bush, Roger D. Masters, and Christopher Kelly (Hanover, NH: University Press of New England, 1992), 149 and 222.

3. Rousseau, *Emile*, 479.

4. Cf. Jacques Derrida, *Of Grammatology*, trans. Gayatri Chakravorty Spivak (Baltimore: Johns Hopkins University Press, 1997), 165ff. Rousseau, *Emile*, 313.

5. Rousseau, *Émile*, vol. 4 of *Œuvres complètes*, ed. Bernard Gagnebin and Marcel Raymond, Bibliothèque de la Pléiade (Paris: Gallimard, 1969), 1416, note b. [Translated by E. Yampolsky.—Trans.]

6. Rousseau, *Confessions*, 379. [Translation modified.—Trans.]

7. Rousseau, *Essay on the Origin of Languages*, vol. 7 of *The Collected Writings of Rousseau*, trans. and ed. John Scott (Hanover, NH: University Press of New England, 1998), 305.

8. Rousseau, preface to *Discourse on the Origin*, 13.

9. This is the hypothesis proposed by Claude Lévi-Strauss: "The opposition between nature and culture to which I attached much importance at one time . . . now seems to be of primarily methodological importance" (*The Savage Mind*, trans. George Weidenfeld [London: Weidenfeld and Nicolson, 1966], 247, note).

10. Rousseau, preface to *Discourse on the Origin*, 14–15.

11. Ibid., 16. [Translation modified.—Trans.]

12. Rousseau, *Social Contract*, 138.

13. "Let us therefore begin by setting all the facts aside, for they do not affect the question. The Researches which can be undertaken concerning this Subject must not be taken for historical truths, but only for hypothetical and conditional reasonings" (Rousseau, preface to *Discourse on the Origin*, 19).

14. "It would be sad for us to be forced to agree that this distinctive and almost unlimited faculty is the source of all man's misfortunes" (ibid., 26).

15. Ibid., 32. "Besides, general ideas can come into the Mind only with the aid of words, and the understanding grasps them only through propositions. That is one of the reasons why animals can neither formulate such ideas nor ever acquire the perfectibility which depends on them" (ibid.). On this notion of "human" perfectibility as it relates to the acquisition of natural languages, see Rousseau, *Essay on the Origin of Languages*, 293. Cf. de Man, "Metaphor (*Second Discourse*)," *Allegories of Reading*, 135–159.

16. Rousseau, *Discourse on the Origin*, 26.

17. "That it is this faculty which, by dint of time, draws him out of that original condition in which he would pass tranquil and innocent days; that it is this faculty, which, bringing to flower over the centuries his enlightenment and his errors, his vices and his virtues, in the long run makes him the tyrant of himself and of Nature" (ibid.).

18. Ibid., 42.

19. "The more one thinks about it, the more one finds that this state was the least subject to revolutions, the best for man, and that he must have come out of it only by some fatal accident, which for the common utility ought never to have happened" (ibid., 48).

20. The question of possible worlds, which Rousseau raises at precise moments of his demonstration but always in order to compare a state of nature to a state of society, should be analyzed rigorously: "Picture an ideal world similar to ours, yet altogether different. Nature is the same there as on our earth, but its economy is more easily felt, its order more marked, its aspect more admirable. Forms are more elegant, colors more vivid, odors sweeter, all objects more interesting" (Rousseau, *Dialogues*, 9).

21. Rousseau searches for the cause of the dissemblance between humans' actions and their discourses: "I found it in our social order which—at every point contrary to nature, which nothing destroys—tyrannizes over nature constantly and constantly makes nature demand its rights." Rousseau, *Letter to Beaumont*, vol. 9 of *The Collected Writings of Rousseau*, ed. Christopher Kelly and Eve Grace, trans. Christopher Kelly and Judith R. Bush (Hanover, NH: University Press of New England, 2001), 52.

22. This is the conclusion drawn by Rousseau: "It follows from this exposition that inequality, being almost null in the state of Nature, draws its force and growth from the development of our faculties and the progress of the human Mind, and finally becomes stable and legitimate by the establishment of property and Laws" (*Discourse on the Origin*, 67).

23. However, this also raises the question of accomplices, without whom no imposture would be possible: "The first person who, having fenced off a plot of ground, took it into his head to say *this is mine* and found people simple enough to believe him, was the true founder of civil society. . . . Beware of listening to this impostor" (ibid., 43). "The rich above all must have soon felt how disadvantageous to them was a perpetual war in which they alone paid all the costs, and in which the risk of life was common to all while the risk of goods was theirs alone" (ibid., 53).

24. Ibid.

25. Rousseau, *Emile*, 343.

26. "The body politic, like the human body, begins to die at the moment of its birth, and carries within itself the causes of its destruction" (Rousseau, *Social Contract*, 188).

27. Rousseau, *Discourse on the Origin*, 54.

28. Rousseau, *Social Contract*, 141.

29. "Each of us puts his person and all his power in common under the supreme direction of the general will; and in a body we receive each member as an indivisible part of the whole" (ibid., 139).

30. Rousseau, *Discourse on the Origin*, 59–60.

31. Rousseau, *Discourse on Political Economy*, 142.

32. Ibid., 143.

33. Ibid.; See also Rousseau, *Social Contract*, 188.

34. Rousseau, *Social Contract*, first version (Geneva Manuscript), 101, emphasis added. See also *Social Contract*, 155.

35. "Through the social compact we have given the body politic existence and life; the issue now is to give it movement and will through legislation. For the original act which forms and unites this body does not thereby determine anything about what it should do to preserve itself" (ibid., 152).

36. Ibid., 103. "Thus one finds combined in the work of legislation two things that seem incompatible: an undertaking beyond human force and, to execute it, an authority that amounts to nothing." Ibid., 156.

37. Ibid., 156.

38. Cf. Bennington, *Dudding: Des noms de Rousseau*, 45–46.

39. Rousseau, *Social Contract*, 195.

40. "But it is this very thing that makes such a Government inadequate in certain respects, because the things that ought to be distinguished are not, and the Prince and the Sovereign, being nothing but the same person, form so to speak only a Government without a Government" (ibid., 173).

41. Ibid., 174.

42. Ibid., 197.

43. "The peculiar advantage of Democratic Government is that it can be established in reality by a simple act of the general will. After this, the provisional Government remains in office, if such is the form adopted, or establishes in the name of the Sovereign the Government prescribed by law; and thus everything is according to rule. It is not possible to institute the Government in any other legitimate way without renouncing the principles established above" (ibid., 196).

44. "But it is not every man who can make the Gods speak or be believed when he declares himself their interpreter. The Legislator's great soul is the true miracle that should prove his mission" (ibid., 157).

45. Ibid., 164–165, emphasis added.

46. Rousseau, *Discourse on Political Economy*, 149.

47. Rousseau, *Social Contract*, 217.

48. Rousseau, *Letters Written from the Mountain*, 147. Cf. Ghislain Waterlot, *Rousseau: Religion et politique* (Paris: Presses universitaires de France, 2004), and André Charrak, "Positions des *Lettres écrites de la montagne. Émile* et le *Contrat social* dans la première lettre," in *Religion, liberté, justice: Sur les "Lettres écrites de la montagne" de Jean-Jacques Rousseau*, ed. Bruno Bernardi, Florent Guénard, and Gabrielle Silvestrini (Paris: Vrin, 2005).

49. Rousseau, *Letters Written from the Mountain*, 148–149.

50. Ibid., 149, note.

51. Ibid., 234.

52. Rousseau, second draft of the preface to *The Levite of Ephraim*, vol. 7 of *The Collected Writings of Rousseau*, trans. and ed. John Scott (Hanover, NH: University Press of New England, 1998), 352. [Translation modified.—Trans.]

53. About this text, see the pertinent analysis by Kamuf, *Signature Pieces*, 100–116.

54. Judges 19:29.

55. "*The Levite of Ephraim*, if it is not the best of my works, will always be the one I cherish most. I have never reread it, I never will reread it, without hearing within me the applause of a heart which knows no rancour, which, far from being embittered by its misfortunes, finds consolation within itself and discovers there the means of its own compensation" (Rousseau, *Confessions*, 574).

56. Rousseau, first draft of the preface to *The Levite of Ephraim*, 351.

57. Rousseau, second draft of the preface to *The Levite of Ephraim*, 352.

58. "He knows that it is not merely the Author he is attacking, but the man; he knows that what he writes can influence my fate. It is no longer only my reputation he has designs upon, but my honor, my freedom, my life" (Rousseau, *Letters Written from the Mountain*, 138).

59. Rousseau, *Dialogues*, 14, emphasis added.

60. Ibid., 6.

61. "But when a clumsy Author, that is to say, an Author who knows his duty, who wants to fulfill it, believes himself obliged to say nothing to the public without avowing it, without naming himself, without showing himself in order to respond, then equity, which ought not to punish the clumsiness of a man of honor as a crime, wants one to proceed with him in another manner. It wants one not to separate the trial of the Book from that of the man, since by putting his name on it he declares that he does not want them separated. It wants one not to judge the work, which cannot respond, until after having heard the Author who responds for it. Thus, although to condemn an anonymous Book might in fact be only to condemn the Book, to condemn a Book that bears the name of the Author, is to condemn the Author himself, and when one does not put him in a position to respond, it is to judge him without having heard him" (Rousseau, *Letters Written from the Mountain*, 219–220).

62. Rousseau, *Dialogues*, 52. [Translation modified.—Trans.]

63. Ibid., 129. Cf. ibid., 65.

64. "I shall in a sense perform on myself the sort of experiments that physicists perform on air to analyse its state day by day. I shall apply the barometer to my soul, and these experiments, conducted well and repeated time and time again, might yield results as reliable as theirs" (Rousseau, *Reveries*, First Walk, 9). [Translation modified.—Trans.]

65. "But they exhausted all their resources in advance: by leaving me with nothing, they have robbed themselves of everything. They have heaped upon me insults, disparagement, mockery, and shame, but these are no more capable of being increased than of being relieved; they are as incapable of making them any worse as I am of escaping them. They were so eager to reduce me to my most wretched state that the whole of human power, even abetted by all the tricks of hell, could not now add to my wretchedness any further" (ibid., 4–5).

66. Ibid., 4.

67. Ibid. "For a long time I put up a fight that was as fierce as it was futile. By fighting without cunning, without skill, without deceit, without caution, frankly, openly, impatiently, and angrily, I managed simply to ensnare myself further and constantly gave them new holds over me which they were careful to exploit" (ibid.).

68. "When I wrote my earliest *Confessions* and my *Dialogues*, I was constantly concerned with finding ways of keeping them out of the clutches of my persecutors, so that I might be able to pass them on to later generations" (ibid., 9).

69. Ibid. [Translation modified.—Trans.]

70. Ibid., 6. [Translation modified.—Trans.]

71. Ibid., 5, emphasis added. "I have found in this resignation the cure for all my ills through the peace of mind that it gives me and which was incompatible with continually pursuing a struggle that was as agonizing as it was ineffectual" (ibid., 4).

72. Ibid., Second Walk, 18.

73. Ibid., 14. "It alone gave me some feeling of myself. In that instant I was born into life, and it seemed to me as if I was filling all the things I saw with my frail existence."

74. Ibid., First Walk, 8. [Translation modified.—Trans.]

75. On fictions as fables, see ibid., Fourth Walk, 38.

76. Ibid., Fifth Walk, 57. "But at least they will not stop me from transporting myself there every day on the wings of my imagination and tasting for a few hours the same pleasure as if I were still living there. The sweetest thing I would do there would be to dream at my leisure. By dreaming that I am there, am I not doing that very thing? I am in fact doing more: to the attraction of an abstract and monotonous reverie I am able to add charming images which enliven it. . . . I am often more in their midst and more pleasurably so than I was when I was really there" (ibid., 57–58).

77. Rousseau, *Discourse on the Origin*, 13.

78. Rousseau, *Reveries*, Eighth Walk, 93. And this is where the question of the state reappears: "I have described this state in one of my reveries. It suits me so well that I desire nothing other than for it to last, and my only fear is seeing it disturbed" (ibid.). This state of survival, between its instant and its duration, its point and its line, merits serious analysis: "These brief moments of madness and passion, however intense they may be, are, precisely because of their very intensity, only ever scattered points along the line of our life. They are too rare and too fleeting to constitute a proper state of being, and the happiness that my heart longs for is not made up of short-lived moments, but of a simple and lasting state, which has nothing intense about it in itself, but which is all the more charming because it lasts, so much so that it finally offers the height of happiness" (ibid., Fifth Walk, 54–55).

79. See n. 66 above.

80. Cf. Jacques Derrida, *Memoires for Paul de Man*, trans. Cecile Lindsay, Jonathan Culler, and Eduardo Cadava (New York: Columbia University Press, 1986), 47–49.

BIBLIOGRAPHY

Works by Jean-Jacques Rousseau

Rousseau, Jean-Jacques. *The Banterer*. Vol. 12 of *The Collected Writings of Rousseau*. Translated and edited by Christopher Kelly. Hanover, NH: University Press of New England, 2007.

———. *Biographical Fragment*. Vol. 12 of *The Collected Writings of Rousseau*. Translated and edited by Christopher Kelly. Hanover, NH: University Press of New England, 2007.

———. *Confessions*. Translated by Angela Scholar. Oxford: Oxford University Press, 2000.

———. *Dialogues: On the Subject and Form of This Writing*. Vol. 1 of *The Collected Writings of Rousseau*. Edited by Roger D. Masters and Christopher Kelly. Translated by Judith R. Bush, Roger D. Masters, and Christopher Kelly. Hanover, NH: University Press of New England, 1990.

———. *Discourse on Political Economy*. Vol. 3 of *The Collected Writings of Rousseau*. Edited by Roger D. Masters and Christopher Kelly. Translated by Judith R. Bush, Roger D. Masters, and Christopher Kelly. Hanover, NH: University Press of New England, 1992.

———. *Discourse on the Origin and Foundations of Inequality among Men*. In *The First and Second Discourses*. Edited by Roger D. Masters .Translated by Roger D. Masters and Judith R. Masters. Boston: Bedford/St. Martin's, 1964.

———. *Discourse on the Origin and Foundations of Inequality among Men (Second Discourse)*. Vol. 3 of *The Collected Writings of Rousseau*. Edited by Roger D. Masters and Christopher Kelly. Translated by Judith R. Bush, Roger D. Masters, Christopher Kelly, and Terrence Marshall. Hanover, NH: University Press of New England, 1992.

———. *Discourse on the Sciences and Arts*. Vol. 2 of *The Collected Writings of Rousseau*. Edited by Roger D. Masters and Christopher Kelly. Translated by Judith R. Bush, Roger D. Masters, and Christopher Kelly. Hanover, NH: University Press of New England, 1992.

———. *Du contrat social*. Vol. 3 of *Œuvres complètes*. Edited by Bernard Gagnebin and Marcel Raymond. Bibliothèque de la Pléiade. Paris: Gallimard, 1964.

———. *Émile*. Vol. 4 of *Œuvres complètes*. Edited by Bernard Gagnebin and Marcel Raymond. Bibliothèque de la Pléiade. Paris: Gallimard, 1969.

———. *Emile, or On Education*. Vol. 13 of *The Collected Writings of Rousseau*. Edited by Christopher Kelly. Translated by Allan Bloom and Christopher Kelly. Hanover, NH: University Press of New England, 2010.

———. *Essay on the Origin of Languages*. Vol. 7 of *The Collected Writings of Rousseau*. Translated and edited by John Scott. Hanover, NH: University Press of New England, 1998.

———. *History of the Preceding Writing*. Vol. 1 of *The Collected Writings of Rousseau*. Edited by Roger D. Masters and Christopher Kelly. Translated by Judith R. Bush, Roger D. Masters, and Christopher Kelly. Hanover, NH: University Press of New England, 1990.

———. *Julie, or The New Heloise*. Vol. 6 of *The Collected Writings of Rousseau*. Edited by Jean Vaché. Translated and annotated by Philip Stewart and Jean Vaché. Hanover, NH: University Press of New England, 1997.

———. *Letter to Beaumont.* Vol. 9 of *The Collected Writings of Rousseau.* Edited by Christopher Kelly and Eve Grace. Translated by Christopher Kelly and Judith R. Bush. Hanover, NH: University Press of New England, 2001.

———. *Letters to Malesherbes.* Vol. 5 of *The Collected Writings of Rousseau.* Edited by Christopher Kelly, Roger D. Masters, and Peter G. Stillman. Translated by Christopher Kelly. Hanover, NH: University Press of New England, 1998.

———. *Letters Written from the Mountain.* Vol. 9 of *The Collected Writings of Rousseau.* Edited by Christopher Kelly and Eve Grace. Translated by Christopher Kelly and Judith R. Bush. Hanover, NH: University Press of New England, 2001.

———. *The Levite of Ephraim.* Vol. 7 of *The Collected Writings of Rousseau.* Translated and edited by John Scott. Hanover, NH: University Press of New England, 1998.

———. *My Portrait.* Vol. 12 of *The Collected Writings of Rousseau.* Translated and edited by Christopher Kelly. Hanover, NH: University Press of New England, 2007.

———. *The Neuchâtel Preface to the "Confessions" of J.-J. Rousseau.* Vol. 5 of *The Collected Writings of Rousseau.* Edited by Christopher Kelly, Roger D. Masters, and Peter G. Stillman. Translated by Christopher Kelly. Hanover, NH: University Press of New England, 1998.

———. *Notes for the Reveries.* Vol. 12 of *The Collected Writings of Rousseau.* Translated and edited by Christopher Kelly. Hanover, NH: University Press of New England, 2007.

———. *On the Art of Enjoying and Other Fragments.* Vol. 12 of *The Collected Writings of Rousseau.* Translated and edited by Christopher Kelly. Hanover, NH: University Press of New England, 2007.

———. *Reveries of the Solitary Walker.* Translated by Russell Goulbourne. Oxford: Oxford University Press, 2011.

———. *Rousseau, Judge of Jean-Jacques: Dialogues.* Vol. 1 of *The Collected Writings of Rousseau.* Edited by Roger D. Masters and Christopher Kelly. Translated by Judith R. Bush, Roger D. Masters, and Christopher Kelly. Hanover, NH: University Press of New England, 1990.

———. *Social Contract.* Vol. 4 of *The Collected Writings of Rousseau.* Edited by Roger D. Masters and Christopher Kelly. Translated by Judith R. Bush, Roger D. Masters, and Christopher Kelly. Hanover, NH: University Press of New England, 1994.

Other Works Cited

Augustine. *Lying.* In *Saint Augustine: Treatises on Various Subjects.* Edited by Roy Deferrari. Translated by Sarah Muldowney. Washington, DC: Catholic University of America Press, 2002.

Barthes, Roland. "The Death of the Author." In *Image, Music, Text.* Translated by S. Heath. London: Fontana, 1977.

Bennington, Geoffrey. *Dudding: Des noms de Rousseau.* Paris: Galilée, 1991.

The Bible. New Revised Standard Version. Washington, DC: National Council of Churches, 1989.

Charrak, André. "Le récit de Rousseau comme épreuve de la liberté de conscience." *Revue de synthèse* 3–4 (1996): 425–439.

———. "Positions des *Lettres écrites de la montagne: Émile* et le *Contrat social* dans la pre-mière lettre." In *Religion, liberté, justice: Sur les "Lettres écrites de la montagne" de Jean-Jacques Rousseau.* Edited by Bruno Bernardi, Florent Guénard, and Gabrielle Silvestrini. Paris: Vrin, 2005.

Chrysostom, John. *On the Priesthood*. Translated by W. R. W. Stephens. Select Library of Nicene and Post Nicene Fathers, ser. 1, vol. 9, edited by Ph. Schaff. London: T. & T. Clark, 1889.

De Man, Paul. *Allegories of Reading*. New Haven, CT: Yale University Press, 1979.

Derrida, Jacques. *Memoires for Paul de Man*. Translated by Cecile Lindsay, Jonathan Culler, and Eduardo Cadava. New York: Columbia University Press, 1986.

———. *Of Grammatology*. Translated by Gayatri Chakravorty Spivak. Baltimore: Johns Hopkins University Press, 1997.

———. "Typewriter Ribbon: Limited Ink (2)." In *Without Alibi*, 71–160. Edited, translated, and with an introduction by Peggy Kamuf. Stanford: Stanford University Press, 2002.

Foucault, Michel. Introduction to *Rousseau juge de Jean-Jacques: Dialogues*, by Jean-Jacques Rousseau. Paris: Armand Colin, 1962.

Gouhier, Henri. *Les méditations métaphysiques de Jean-Jacques Rousseau*. Paris: Vrin, 1985.

Hilary of Poitiers. *Traité des mystères (Tractatus mysteriorum)*. Edited and translated by J.-P. Brisson. Paris: Le Cerf, 1947.

Kamuf, Peggy. *Signature Pieces: On the Institution of Authorship*. Ithaca, NY: Cornell University Press, 1988.

Kant, Immanuel. *Grounding for the Metaphysics of Morals: On a Supposed Right to Lie Because of Philanthropic Concerns*. 1797. Translated by James W. Ellington. Indianapolis, IN: Hackett, 1993.

Lacan, Jacques. "The Direction of the Treatment and the Principles of Its Power." In *Écrits*. Translated by Bruce Fink. New York: Norton, 2007.

Lévi-Strauss, Claude. *The Savage Mind*. Translated by George Weidenfeld. London: Weidenfeld and Nicolson, 1966.

Margel, Serge. "*Mendacium est fabula* ou le droit de mentir par aveu d'innocence. Jean-Jacques Rousseau: de la IVe *Rêverie* à l'exergue des *Confessions*." *Archives de philosophies* 63 (2000): 5–29.

Nietzsche, Friedrich. "On Truth and Lying." 1873. In *Friedrich Nietzsche on Rhetoric and Language*. Edited and translated with a critical introduction by Sander L. Gilman, Carole Blair, and David J. Parent. New York: Oxford University Press, 1989.

Pindar. *Nemean*. In *Nemean Odes; Isthmian Odes; Fragments*. Edited and translated by William H. Race. Loeb Classical Library 485. Cambridge, MA: Harvard University Press, 1997.

———. *Pythians*. In *Olympian Odes; Pythian Odes*. Edited and translated by William H. Race. Loeb Classical Library 56. Cambridge, MA: Harvard University Press, 1997.

Plato. *Laws, Books 1–6*. Translated by R. G. Bury. Loeb Classical Library 187. Cambridge, MA: Harvard University Press, 1926.

———. *Lesser Hippias*. In *Cratilus; Parmenides; Greater Hippias; Lesser Hippias*. Translated by Harold North Fowler. Loeb Classical Library 167. Cambridge, MA: Harvard University Press, 1926.

———. *Republic, Books 1–5*. Edited and translated by Christopher Emlyn-Jones and William Preddy. Loeb Classical Library 237. Cambridge, MA: Harvard University Press, 2013.

———. *Statesman*. In *Statesman; Philebus; Ion*. Translated by Harold North Fowler and W. R. M. Lamb. Loeb Classical Library 164. Cambridge, MA: Harvard University Press, 1925.

Sartre, Jean-Paul. *Being and Nothingness*. Translated and with an introduction by Hazel E. Barnes. New York: Washington Square Press, 1992.

Sinapi, Michèle. "Le mensonge officieux dans la correspondance Jérôme-Augustin." *Rue Descartes* 8–9 (1993): 63–83.

Starobinski, Jean. *Jean-Jacques Rousseau: La transparence et l'obstacle*. Paris: Gallimard, 1970.
———. *Rousseau: Transparency and Obstruction*. Translated by Arthur Goldhammer. Chicago: University of Chicago Press, 1988.
———. *The Living Eye*. Translated by Arthur Goldhammer. Cambridge, MA: Harvard University Press, 1989.
Waterlot, Ghislain. *Rousseau: Religion et politique*. Paris: Presses universitaires de France, 2004.

INDEX

SERGE MARGEL is a philosopher and philologist who teaches at the University of Neuchâtel, Switzerland. He is the author of numerous books and articles on the relations between literature, art, and philosophy. Several of his works have been translated into English, including *The Tomb of the Artisan God: On Plato's Timaeus.*

EVA YAMPOLSKY has a PhD in French literature from Emory University and a PhD in the history of medicine from the University of Lausanne, Switzerland. She has published, edited, and translated works on literature, medicine, and philosophy.

www.ingramcontent.com/pod-product-compliance
Lightning Source LLC
Chambersburg PA
CBHW030309100426
42812CB00002B/636